COLLEGE LIBRARY
ST.
JOSEPH'S
COLLEGE
1852
Phila., Pa.

Learning How to Behave

·The M Co·

THE MACMILLAN COMPANY
NEW YORK · BOSTON · CHICAGO
DALLAS · ATLANTA · SAN FRANCISCO

MACMILLAN AND CO., LIMITED
LONDON · BOMBAY · CALCUTTA
MADRAS · MELBOURNE

THE MACMILLAN COMPANY
OF CANADA, LIMITED
TORONTO

Learning How to Behave

A HISTORICAL STUDY OF AMERICAN ETIQUETTE BOOKS

By Arthur M. Schlesinger

1947

THE MACMILLAN COMPANY · NEW YORK

Second printing.

PRINTED IN THE UNITED STATES OF AMERICA

CONTENTS

	Introduction	vii
I.	First Lessons	1
II.	Progress in the Northern Ports	8
III.	Republican Etiquette	15
IV.	The Cult of Elegance	27
V.	Relax!	49
VI.	The Balance Sheet	62
	Acknowledgments	72
	Bibliography and Notes	74
	Index	91

INTRODUCTION

FOR SOME PEOPLE THE SUBJECT OF ETIQUETTE IS TAINTED WITH SNOBBERY. IF THEY HAD THEIR WAY, THE TRUE DEMOCRAT would treat it with contempt and Clio consider it beneath her dignity. Yet nothing that concerns human beings can fail to concern the historian, men's foibles as well as their virtues. The rise and progress of courtesy would, if for no other reason, merit interest as a sort of barometer of changing attitudes toward greater affairs, but it also deserves attention for its own sake as a functional trait of civilization. Manners, far from being apart from life, are veritably a part of life, revealing men's hopes, standards and strivings. This is particularly true of the United States, a new country in the eyes of the Old World and one settled by those plain people whom Lincoln said the Lord must love because He made so many of them. How did Tom, Dick and Harry set about to acquire the decencies and self-respecting ways of Thomas, Richard and Henry? The true democrat may well hearken to the story, for, viewed from this angle, the gyrations of the fashionable and giddy become a mere sideshow. What is involved is an illuminating phase of the leveling-up process of democracy.

In struggling toward this goal the American people have

been hampered historically by five conditions. The first was the fact that the colonies were settled in the main by persons who in the Old World had been cut off from the usages of the best society. The second was the absence of a native hereditary aristocracy, which might, as in Europe, have served to set standards of taste and deportment; instead, a succession of classes rose to the top. A third hindrance consisted in the necessity of taming a wilderness before cultivating the graces of living, a need constantly renewed as the nation shifted westward toward the Pacific. The situation was complicated further by the incoming of hordes of immigrants, people who faced all the difficulties common to the native-born as well as the additional one of having to master the unfamiliar customs of their English-speaking neighbors.

Finally, an essential support to good manners appeared wanting in the comparative fewness of women. In Western Europe, where they usually outnumbered the men, they had proved the principal guardians of decorum in the middle and upper ranks of society, but in America, as in all new countries, women formed a minority and it seemed hardly possible for them to play their traditional role.

As it turned out, however, the relative scarcity of the one sex had the effect of enhancing its value in the eyes of the other and caused men to compete in politeness for feminine favor. The results, of course, fell short of the ceremonial demeanor characteristic of the best European circles, but something was substituted which the older civilization lacked. "From the captain of a western steamboat to the roughest miner in California, from north, south, east and west," wrote a nineteenth-century commentator, "we hear but one voice. Women are to be protected, respected, supported and petted." [1] The same voice had been heard in the earliest days of settlement. From first to last, foreign observers never failed to record their astonishment that lone women could travel in all parts of the country without fear of molestation or insult. In this chivalry of men lay at least the starting point for attaining a greater sophistication of manners.

If the undersupply of women proved a lesser obstacle than might have been expected, the other impediments were also overcome in the course of time. The story of the accomplishment can be told here only in broad outline. The account has its mirthful moments, but the reader who smiles should smile with compassion, for he is witnessing one aspect of the common man's struggle to achieve a larger degree of human dignity and self-respect.

FIRST LESSONS

THE VAST BULK OF THE COLONISTS, COMING FROM THE PEASANT AND WORKING CLASSES, BROUGHT WITH THEM NO TRADITION of polite behavior to temper and gild the crudities of existence in the New World. Happily, the religious atmosphere exerted a softening influence, for the seventeenth and eighteenth centuries equated morals with religion and commonly identified manners with morals. Besides, the more substantial settlers—the minority who wielded political and economic power—possessed a pride of station that made them want to develop in the wilderness something approaching the English aristocratic system. A graded society would give them a status which few of them had enjoyed in the mother country. It would, moreover, ensure a harmonious relationship of classes according to the age-old European pattern.

At the bottom layers of the community the legislatures and courts enforced minimum standards of civility, just as in Britain during these same years. In this respect no marked differences existed between Puritan New England, Quaker Pennsylvania and the provinces farther south.[1] People were punished, usually in public, for scandalmongering, cursing, lying, name-calling, even for flirting, jeering, "finger-sticking" and making ugly faces. Swains who won the affections of maids without parental consent risked fines of from five to ten pounds with costs. A gossip or scold might be exhibited with tongue pinched in a cleft stick or, as in Massachusetts, be "Gagged, or set in a Ducking stool, and dipt over Head and Ears three times in some convenient place of fresh or salt water." [2] Profane persons and drunkards were consigned to the stocks, when not whipped like slanderers and the perpetrators of insults. The object of these penalties was not merely to chasten the offender, but to dramatize for onlookers the consequences of gross breaches of decorum.

That this correctional system was designed mainly for the poor is indicated sometimes by the wording of the legislation and even more patently by the enforcement. An early Virginia act provided that any man or woman who aroused matrimonial hopes simultaneously in two members of the opposite sex should be disciplined "according to the quality of the person so offending." In general, society tended to regard the pillory and branding with a hot iron as more polished forms of punishment than the stocks or flogging. The legal prescriptions as to dress, common to Virginia, Massachusetts and Connecticut during much of the seventeenth century, seemed to waver between the purpose of sharpening class distinctions and that of preventing extravagant expenditures even by the high-toned.[3] Thus a Massachusetts statute of 1651 forbidding "men and women of meane condition" to wear gold or silver lace and silk scarves was followed by another in 1675 condemning "the evil of pride in Apparrel, both for Costliness in the poorer sort, and vain, new strange Fashions both in poor and rich." Connecticut likewise deemed such finery "unbecoming a wilderness condition and the profession of the gospel." In time difficulties of execution caused such regulations to fall into disuse. Even in these olden days fashion had a way of operating according to its own laws.

The clergy joined the government in the Sisyphean task of refining manners, and the publishers of almanacs also lent a hand. Whereas the preachers administered solemn warnings and reproof, the almanac makers dispensed their medicine in savory homeopathic doses, mixing their injunctions with practical information about the weather and daily affairs. Poor Richard, for example, while admitting, "We may give advice, but we cannot give conduct," nevertheless proceeded to offer such apt admonitions as "An undutiful daughter, will make an unmanageable wife"; "None but the well-bred man knows how to confess a fault, or acknowledge himself in error"; "Love your neighbour; yet don't pull down your hedge"; "Keep your eyes wide open before marriage, half shut afterwards"; "Fish and visitors stink in three days"; and "He is not well bred, that cannot bear ill-breeding in others." Nathaniel Ames, another almanac authority, summed up the whole matter by saying, "Good sense is the foundation of good manners," and "Tell me thy Manners and I'll tell thy Fortune." [4]

In the dearth of other reading matter the average person sedulously studied his almanac, and the occasional signposts of deportment he found there helped no doubt to guide his steps in the right direction. For many adults, however, the advice came too late to alter habits already well fixed. To indoctrinate more susceptible minds became a function of the schools, though schools were few as yet, especially outside New England. A New York statute of 1732 echoed a favorite Yankee belief that education was "the properest Means to Attain Knowledge, Improve the Mind, Morality and good Manners." [5]

What children were taught under the last of these headings is probably indicated by the contents of Eleazar Moody's *The School of Good Manners,* a juvenile handbook frequently reprinted during the eighteenth century.[6] As in the case of the adult manuals later described, the reputed author, a Boston schoolmaster, adapted the work from an English version of a French original. The instructions covered conduct in church, at home, in company, at school and on the street. Youngsters were told: "Be not hasty to run out of the meeting-house when the worship is ended"; "Never speak to thy parents without some title of respect, as, *sir, madam,* &c." [7]; "Spit not, cough not, nor blow thy nose at the table, if it may be avoided"; "Among superiors speak not till thou art spoken to"; "If thy superior be relating a story, say not, 'I have heard it before' . . . . If he tell it not right, snigger not"; "Go not singing, whistling or hallooing along the street"; and "Pull off thine hat to persons of desert, quality or office; shew thy reverence to them by bowing thy body."

George Washington, composing his own set of rules in 1747 at the age of fifteen, may have been influenced by the *School of Good Manners,* but it is more probable that he borrowed his maxims directly from an English adaptation of another sixteenth-century French guide.[8] In any event, the hundred and ten precepts represented usages which the best social mentors of the time would have sanctioned. Of behavior in company he wrote: "Reprehend not the imperfections of others for that belongs to Parents, Masters and Superiours"; "Contradict not at every turn what others Say"; "In Speaking to men of Quality do not lean nor Look them full in the Face." When dining, "Put not another bit into your mouth til the former be Swallowed"; "Cleanse not your teeth with the Table Cloth, Napkin, Fork or Knife." As for other matters of decorum, "Wear not your Cloths, foul, unript or Dusty"; "Spit not in the Fire"; "Kill no Vermin as Fleas, lice ticks &c in the Sight of Others." And for the final entry young Washington wrote, "Labour to keep alive in your Breast that Little Spark of Celestial fire Called Conscience." [9]

Both the *School of Good Manners* and Washington's "Rules of Civility" aimed at a more advanced code of conduct than that for which the lawmakers and the almanac makers strove. This rising interest in good form or etiquette reflected the desire of certain groups to imitate the better classes at home. The means lay at hand, for the English aristocracy itself had long been engaged in learning correct behavior from France, which since the age of chivalry had been Europe's chief instructor in courtesy. For many years the most popular British manuals of deportment were translations, revisions or plagiarisms of French guides, with an occasional adaptation from the Italian; and these publications, sometimes in the original tongue, early found their way onto the shelves of well-to-do colonials. Elder William Brewster of Plymouth, for example, owned a treatise by Stefano Guazzo, and among the books of Governor John Winthrop, Jr., of Connecticut was one by Castiglione.[10]

But it was in the South, notably Virginia, that conduct books had the most eager readers, for after the first toilsome years of breaking the wilderness the successful planter, dwelling on his broad acres amidst many black vassals, proceeded deliberately to model his life on that of the English landed gentry. The Virginian, William Fitzhugh of Stafford County, spoke for his kind when he said in 1687 that his children had "better be never born than illbred." [11]

Such seventeenth-century English manuals as Henry Peacham's *The Compleat Gentleman,* Richard Brathwaite's *The English Gentleman* and Richard Allestree's *The Whole Duty of Man* afforded the necessary guidance. Thomas Jefferson numbered *The Whole Duty* among his books, and in 1764 George Washington, untiring in his efforts for self-improvement, acquired a Williamsburg reprint of the work.[12] Women too had to learn to do the honors of their station, for on their shoulders plantation life laid heavy domestic and social responsibilities. Allestree's *The Ladies Calling* (1673) was their mainstay, but numerous aids were available in other imported handbooks like Lord Halifax's *The Lady's New Year's Gift: or, Advice to a Daughter* (1688), the anonymous *Ladies Library* (1714) and Abbé d'Ancourt's *The Lady's Preceptor* (1743).[13]

For the Southern aristocracy this literature provided a fairly consistent chart of behavior—something to aspire to if not always to attain. In emulation of the ancient ideals of Christian chivalry the writers held up valor, probity, justice, piety and courtesy as the earmarks of a gentleman, and modesty, chastity, meekness, godliness and compassion as the traits of a lady. A gentlewoman should refer all offers of marriage to her parents and after wedlock render her husband unquestioning obedience. If he was a philanderer, she should, in the words of Lord Halifax, "affect ignorance" of his infidelities; if he was ill-natured, she must avoid provoking him; if a drunkard, she should rejoice that this failing offset her own many shortcomings; if feeble-minded, then—lucky female—she could cut "a better Figure, for her Husband's making no great one."

As time went on, the manuals gave increasing attention to the ceremonious aspects of social intercourse. In particular, the distaff side was instructed what to wear, how to arrange a dinner, what diversions to seek and how to converse in company ("Women seldom have Materials to furnish a long Discourse"). One French traveler, unfortunate perhaps in his hosts, felt obliged to report that the Virginia planters "do not understand the use of napkins, that they wear silk scarves, and that instead of using handkerchiefs they blow their noses with their fingers, or with a silk handkerchief which serves as a cravat, napkin, etc.," but he was the exception.[14] The great majority of European visitors found Southern society the most urbane in America.

PROGRESS IN THE NORTHERN PORTS

AS A PROSPEROUS CLASS OF MERCHANTS AND TRADESMEN IN THE NORTHERN PORTS PARALLELED THE RISE OF THE PLANTING aristocracy in the South, they made a similar effort to behave as befitted their station. They represented that element in the community which in later times would set the standards for the nation, but as yet they had not discovered the virtues of conspicuous waste and busy idleness, and the handbooks on which they relied, like those in the South, emphasized manners in their aspect of "minor morals."

Cotton Mather's *Ornaments for the Daughters of Zion* (1692), for example, enlarged upon Tertullian's injunction: "Cloath your selves with the *Silk* of Piety, the *Satin* of Sanctity, the *Purple* of Modesty; So the Almighty God will be a *Lover* of you." [1] Benjamin Franklin, resting his case on ethics rather than religion, put forth his *Reflections on Courtship and Marriage* (1746) which, in amplifying Poor Richard's occasional hints on the subject, cast doubt on the accepted views as to the inequality of the sexes. Blaming man for many of woman's inadequacies, he counseled that both husband and wife be on their best behavior toward each other and that the husband should rule the roost only if he were the more sensible of the two. Franklin's treatise, anonymously written, was in advance of the times, but it achieved three more American editions in thirteen years besides one at Edinburgh.[2]

Manuals of native authorship, however, were the exception rather than the rule. In fact, the habit of looking to England for social tutelage continued for a good half century after the severing of political bonds. Occasionally some of the popular Southern guides were consulted in the North. Franklin himself urged that his daughter Sally read *The Whole Duty of Man* and *The Ladies Library* "over and over again." [3] But most of the Northern favorites were of later vintage and apparently found few readers among the plantation gentry.

From Philadelphia to Boston the newspapers advertised these imported volumes, and as the eighteenth century waxed older, printers in the principal Northern towns, taking the tide at the flood, got out their own editions of the works.[4] Judged by frequency of republication, the best sellers were *The Friendly Instructor,* reprinted six times between 1745 and 1750 and twice more in the 1790's; William Kenrick's *The Whole Duty of a Woman; or, a Guide to the Female Sex, from the Age of Sixteen to Sixty,* ten American editions, 1761–1798; W. H. Dilworth's *The Complete Letter-Writer,* thirteen in the same period; [5] John Gregory's *A Father's Legacy to His Daughters,* twenty-seven, 1775–1798; Lord Chesterfield's *Letters to His Son,* at least thirty-one, 1775–1800, though with variations of title and text; Hester M. Chapone's *Letters on the Improvement of the Mind,* six, 1783–1797; and John Bennet's *Letters to a Young Lady,* six in the 1790's.[6]

Chesterfield's work apart, this host of courtesy books did

little more than underline the moralistic and religious teachings which had inspired the older treatises still persisting in the South. A woman's chief function in life was to comport herself in such a way as to entrap a man and so attain earth's greatest bliss, matrimony, and an eventual shoal of children. Wit, warned Dr. Gregory, was the most dangerous talent a girl could have; she should be cautious even about displaying good sense; and if she happened to be well educated, she must "keep it a profound secret, especially from the men, who generally look with a jealous and malignant eye on a woman of great parts, and a cultivated understanding." [7]

The Reverend John Bennet, getting down to cases, told his female readers, "Politics, philosophy, mathematics, or metaphysics, are not *your* province. Machiavel, Newton, Euclid, Malebranche, or Locke, will lie with a very ill grace in your closets." With equal care they should avoid powder, perfume and cosmetics and strive only for neatness and simplicity in dress ("Be content to be what God and nature *intended* you"). It was pardonable, though, for a young lady to divert herself with "a walk, a ride, a book [provided it was neither a novel nor too learned], a garden, or the society of a chosen [feminine] friend." [8] When the supreme moment came, she should not marry against her parents' wishes nor, in the opinion of most authorities, against her own. Gregory, however, maintained that her "greater flexibility of taste" rendered love an irrelevant consideration.[9] Once having taken the step, she must, of course, evince toward her husband that "consciousness of *inferiority,* which, for the sake of *order,* the all-wise Author of nature *manifestly* intended." [10]

The Earl of Chesterfield, however, expounded strikingly different principles of behavior, and nonchalantly tore from women their last shreds of self-respect, his passages on the sex culminating in the instructions to his son on how to set about seducing certain Parisian ladies of fashion. In Chesterfield's view good breeding was founded not upon consideration for others, as the moralists taught, but upon consideration for self. It was a technique of dissimulation for getting ahead in the world or, to use a modern phrase, for winning friends and influencing people. "Those necessary connections," he wrote, "can never be formed, or preserved, but by an uninterrupted series of complaisance, attentions, politeness, and some constraint," and to that end the youth should make it his "only care" every evening from dinner to bedtime to cultivate the "thousand little delicacies, which are established by custom."

He must not talk bluntly to equals or insolently to inferiors. He must never argue in company, or comport himself otherwise than quietly ("Well-bred people often smile, but seldom laugh"). It was equally ill-advised to indulge in such habits as grabbing the best chair, blowing one's nose without a handkerchief, eating with a knife or using a fork to pick one's teeth. On the other hand, manly frailties arising from high spirits and warm blood, such as "a gallantry, an accidental excess of the table, a frolic," were allowable. "Dress," Chesterfield conceded, "is a very foolish thing; and yet it is a very foolish thing for a man not to be well dressed, according to his rank and way of life." Women too had their uses, even apart from amatory adventures, for their companionship polished masculine manners and they might have friends in influential quarters. To be sure, "a man of sense only trifles with them, plays with them, humours and flatters them, as he does with a sprightly forward child. . . . No flattery is either too high or too low for them." [11]

In the unexpurgated form in which this worldly-wise disquisition first reached America it aroused deep indignation. Mrs. John Adams, who had gladly accepted Dr. Benjamin Rush's gift of a copy of John Gregory's *A Father's Legacy,* raged against Lord Chesterfield for "inculcateing the most immoral, pernicious and Libertine principals into the mind of a youth" at the same time that he taught him "to wear the outward garb of virtue." [12] Bennet, voicing the middle-class sentiments of the United States as well as of his own country, said "every woman in the world" had reason to execrate the author, and wondered, "If this writer had not been a peer, who would have read his letters with so much avidity?" [13]

But even Abigail Adams admitted that "many excellent maxims and rules for the conduct of youth" were strewn through the work; and it was this fact on which American publishers promptly seized, getting out versions which excised the improprieties while capitalizing upon the author's snob appeal. Usually rebaptized *Principles of Politeness,* Chesterfield's prolix discourse was "methodised and digested under distinct headings," and, so denatured, it quickly topped all other manuals in popularity.[14] The adjective "Chesterfieldian" passed into the language, shedding its offensive implications and bestowing the accolade of exceptional courtliness of bearing.

The continued repute of British courtesy books through the tumultuous years of Revolutionary agitation and armed strife and during the early decades of the Republic suggests how little political separation affected subservience to the parent country in matters of decorum. To be sure, the Reverend Enos Hitchcock, in a work dedicated to Martha Washington, exhorted his countrymen to assert independence in manners, customs, education and dress as well as in government; and a writer in the *American Museum,* probably reflecting gratitude for France's timely aid in the war, urged the superiority of Gallic social usages to "many disgusting, embarrassing, destructive English customs." [15] In fact, translations of a few French treatises enjoyed a temporary vogue, notably Pierre Joseph Boudier de Villemert's *The Ladies' Friend,* which ran through seven editions between 1782 and 1795. But ingrained habit favored the time-honored ways, and as long as the class structure of the population continued without substantial change, no departures seemed likely.

The flight of many thousands of well-to-do Tories, traditional exemplars of genteel living, had no apparent effect on manners, nor did any bad consequences appear to arise from the action of the states in relaxing or revoking the ancient penalties for blatant breaches of civility among the common herd. This step, taken in response to the humanitarian impulses of the Revolutionary movement, probably indicated also a recognition of a general improvement of deportment resulting from the steady advance in economic and social status since the early days of settlement.

The more popular of the older British guides continued to

be reissued during the first quarter of the nineteenth century along with occasional imitative manuals by native authors. The decade after 1806 saw six new editions of Chesterfield added to the thirty-one or more that had been published earlier. Several years later, in 1827, the work completed the final formality of naturalization by being offered to the public as *The American Chesterfield*.[16]

REPUBLICAN ETIQUETTE

A SOCIAL CODE, LIKE A GARMENT ON THE HUMAN BODY, OUTLIVES ITS USEFULNESS WHEN IT NO LONGER FITS THE FORM FOR which it was designed. Its acceptability at any given time rests upon the willingness of the well-mannered to adhere to it and of most other people to look up to it. If class relations change, so also must the canons of breeding or else forfeit every vestige of authority; and it follows that the more violent the change, the more imperative is the need for compromise and adjustment.

Such a challenge confronted American manners in the second quarter of the nineteenth century. Many things conspired to undermine ancient attitudes and upset hallowed landmarks. The War of 1812, misinterpreted as a glorious victory, exalted the self-confidence of the postwar generation. The extension of the nation's authority to the Rio Grande and the Pacific, the expanding web of canals and railroads, the outflow of humanity into untenanted areas, the springing up of new cities in the older regions, the rapid technological progress and notable growth of industry—all these bred in Americans the sense of a mighty people marching toward a goal such as mankind had never known. And with these developments went others more subtle in character: the steady rise of countless humble folk to higher living standards, and the admission of all white men to the ballot and the right to hold office. These altered conditions could not fail to leave their mark on social usages, particularly in the North where their principal impact was felt.

Andrew Jackson's elevation to the White House in 1828 was a political outcropping of deeper human stirrings. The son of a destitute Scotch-Irish immigrant, he had by dint of pluck and native capacity arrived at the seat of power hitherto reserved for the Harvard-educated Adamses and great Virginia landholders. Protagonists of the old order, alarmed by the "millennium of minnows" at Washington, misunderstood the nature of the upsurge that Jackson's election betokened.[1] The dreaded minnows, whether agitating the turbid pool at the federal capital or disturbing the broader waters throughout the land, had no intention of remaining small fry, or even of always swimming with their kind. To them the country's new political and economic situation meant the opportunity for little fish to grow into big ones. "True republicanism," agreed a contemporary, "requires that every man shall have an equal chance—that every man shall be free to become as unequal as he can." [2]

Unlike former times, ordinary folk now felt they could make of themselves what they would. As Catharine Sedgwick reminded them, "It is not here as in the old world, where one man is born with a silver spoon, and another with a pewter one, in his mouth. You may all handle silver spoons, if you will. That is, you may all rise to places of respectability." [3] Though devoting their chief energies to bettering their material lot, they never lost sight of the fact that self-respect also demanded they climb toward higher social levels. The passion for equality, in other words, found expression in the view that all could become gentlemen, not that gentlemen should cease to be. President Jackson himself, despite his lowly origins and the hoary Whig legend in history books of his uncouthness, excited the admiration of both friend and foe by his urbane and courtly demeanor.[4] To be sure, a shirt-sleeve approach to good manners naturally outraged the Southern planter's conception of a properly regulated world. Little wonder that a Georgia aristocrat, writing in the mid-century, found the North "devoid of society fitted for well-bred gentlemen" because so many of the persons he encountered were "mechanics struggling to be genteel." [5]

One of the arguments for sowing the North with little red schoolhouses was that "the first indispensable requisite for good society is *education*"; and though other reasons proved more influential in bringing about public schools, the colonial precedent of using the classroom for instructing the young in civility received the fullest possible application.[6] The states now generally required the teaching of such basic qualities as truthfulness, sobriety, temperance, industry, piety and chastity.[7] Educational leaders further proclaimed it the duty of schoolmasters to make up for any other deficiencies of home training,[8] and textbook writers quickly obliged with sections on "Politeness," "Manners at Table" and "Manners in the Street and on the Road." [9]

Older persons received a certain amount of help from the magazines, especially from *Godey's Lady's Book* and similar women's journals, whose sentimental stories featured heroes and heroines of immaculate gentility, and whose editors sometimes offered specific recipes for social deportment and affairs of the heart. Mrs. James Parton, known to her numerous readers as Fanny Fern, took occasion in her discursive essays—which generally reached a wider public in book form—to include tart comments on ill breeding. Two of her "Rules for Ladies" were: "Always keep callers waiting, till they have had time to notice the outlay of money in your parlors"; and "Always whisper and laugh at concerts, by way of compliment to the performers, and to show your neighbors a sovereign contempt for their comfort." [10]

Such incidental references, however, did not replace the manuals devoted wholly to social decorum, a type of publication which, given the new circumstances of American life, now attained an importance never before known. Mrs. Sarah Josepha Hale, who presided over *Godey's,* considered it one of her bounden duties to recommend these writings as they issued from the press, and in time she produced her own treatise on *Manners; or, Happy Homes and Good Society* (1866).[11] From the late 1820's on, this literature poured forth in a never-ending stream. An incomplete enumeration shows that, aside from frequent revisions and new editions, twenty-eight different manuals appeared in the 1830's, thirty-six in the 1840's and thirty-eight more in the 1850's—an average of over three new ones annually in the pre-Civil War decades.

They not only greatly exceeded the number published at any earlier time, but they were also mostly of American authorship. The writers embraced such persons as Lydia H.

Sigourney and Catharine M. Sedgwick, the novelists; Eliza W. Farrar, biographer of Lafayette and wife of a Harvard professor; William A. Alcott, cousin of Bronson Alcott and an educational reformer; T. S. Arthur, best known today as the author of *Ten Nights in a Bar-room;* and Eliza Leslie, a successful writer of juvenile fiction. Lola Montez, the Irish-Spanish actress who dazzled America in the mid-century, discoursed appropriately enough on *The Arts of Beauty* (1858), graciously including "hints to gentlemen on the art of fascinating." Ralph Waldo Emerson, though not himself a contributor to the genre, lent a certain elevation to the theme by devoting two of his essays to "Manners" and "Behavior." He could even commend his friend Walter Savage Landor for saying, "I have suffered more from my bad dancing than from all the miseries and misfortunes of my life put together." [12]

The conduct books were of two general kinds, one upholding the time-honored conception of manners as "character in action," the other elaborating the view, already rendered familiar by the American adaptations of Chesterfield, that manners are a set of rules to be learned. With the nation passing through a period of unsettling social change, moralists feared lest the ancient pillars of individual integrity and family virtues be destroyed, and they publicized their concern in treatises ascribing true courtesy to "the source of all purity and goodness, the Christian religion." [13] In this spirit William A. Alcott ambitiously attempted to canvass every aspect of personal and domestic relations in *The Young Man's Guide* (1832), *The Young Woman's Guide* (1836), *The*

Young Mother (1836), *The Young Wife* (1837), *The Young Husband* (1838) and *The Boy's Guide* (1844).

Yet neither he nor his less fecund fellow scribes wholly ignored conduct in the more restricted sense of etiquette. George W. Hervey in *The Principles of Courtesy* excused himself for touching on such trivia by the need to counteract the many handbooks that "appealed to unworthy motives, and taught a heartless and selfish system of politeness." [14] Taking somewhat different ground, Alcott argued that a practice like wearing one's hat in the house "tends to vice and immorality." [15] T. S. Arthur, on the other hand, though warning against drawing-room usages based on self-seeking and vanity, frankly urged his readers to study etiquette manuals for their own sake.[16]

Arthur by this advice showed himself far more in accord with the times than were most purveyors of what Fanny Fern called "moral molasses." [17] The rising classes, reasonably confident of their grip on Christian principles but timorous about the proprieties of taste and behavior, thirsted to know "the little things, the graceful finishing touches," which they associated with persons to the manner born. " 'The power of littles!' " wrote Mrs. Hale approvingly. "How often has the expression been quoted, how much it contains!" [18]

Those who set their hands to the task of meeting the demand did so with a clear understanding of the audience they were addressing. "I have seen it gravely stated by some writer on manners, that 'it takes three generations to make a gentleman,' " said the wellborn Miss Sedgwick, and she emphatically rejoined, "This is too slow a process in these days of accelerated movement." As encouragement to the faint-hearted she added, "You have it in your power to fit yourselves by the cultivation of your minds, and the refinement of your manners for intercourse, on equal terms, with the best society in our land." [19]

In the nature of the case, these treatises played pretty much the same tune in pretty much the same way. Some continued to appeal to English or French usages as authority, but the greater number scorned the "stiff and stately pomp of fashion as it comes out of the atmosphere of monarchical courts" and espoused a "truly American and republican school of politeness." Nathaniel P. Willis, a widely read *arbiter elegantiarum,* conferred his approval in the columns of the *Home Journal,* declaring, "We should be glad to see a distinctively American school of good manners, in which all useless etiquettes were thrown aside, but every politeness adopted or invented which could promote sensible and easy exchanges of good will and sensibility. . . . To get rid of *imported superfluities* of etiquette is the first thing to do." [20]

The flag-wavers not only reflected more faithfully the national mood, but they derived a further advantage from the fact that on certain matters of good form the English and the French were at variance, thus forcing Americans at the very least to choose between them.[21] Nevertheless, reprints of certain imported manuals enjoyed an appreciable vogue, especially those tailored to the comparable needs of the rising classes in the homelands.[22] Nearly all the works, whether of foreign or native origin, carefully avoided the old-time references to the etiquette of inferiors toward superiors, one author even deeming it necessary to argue that republican sensitivity did not forbid closing a letter with the formula: "I have the honour to be your very obedient servant." [23]

The handbooks to which the uninitiated turned were generally crisp and to the point, shunning the leisurely epistolary approach of the eighteenth century. The matter was neatly arranged, nothing was taken for granted, and the precepts were so simply phrased as to be easily remembered, or even memorized. The prices charged for the volumes proved a further attraction. Some sold for as little as twenty-five cents, and just before the Civil War the hustling New York firm headed by Irwin P. Beadle published a vastly popular *Dime Book of Practical Etiquette* (1859). To deepen the impression on readers, the writers often spoke as though their advice possessed a quasi-legal sanction. "Politeness and etiquette," said one author, "form a sort of supplement to the law, which enables society to protect itself against offences which the law cannot touch." [24] Another entitled his book *The Laws of Etiquette*, while still another observed in Benthamite phrase, "The Laws of Convention, like all wise laws, are instituted to promote 'the greatest good of the greatest number.' " [25]

Since these missionaries of manners were preaching principally to the social heathen, they did not flinch from expounding first principles. Thus one admonished, "Never sleep in any garment worn during the day." A second inveighed against so-called "genteel people who never use the bath, or only once or twice a year wash themselves all over, though they change their linen daily." A third explained, "A gentleman never sits in the house with his hat on in the presence of ladies for a single moment." [26] By the same token, he should never smoke in their presence, or where they might come, even on the street, and clothing tainted with the fumes must be changed before going into company. The mania of spitting, everywhere and on all occasions, fell under a similar ban. The female reader, for her part, was told it was an offense against decorum to let her overnight hostess "know that you have found or felt insects in your bed." [27] A typical catalogue of bad company manners included the following:

> to balance yourself upon your chair; . . . to extend your feet on the andirons; to admire yourself with complacency in a glass; . . . to laugh immoderately; to place your hand upon the person with whom you are conversing; to take him by the buttons, the collar of his cloak, the cuffs, the waist, &c.; to seize ladies by the waist, or to touch their person; . . . to beat time with the feet and hands; to whirl round a chair on one leg.[28]

The ordeal of dining involved many further traps for the unwary, to which etiquette authorities devoted loving attention. Among the inviolable injunctions were to remove one's gloves before eating; to unfold the napkin and, in the case of a woman, pin it to one's belt; to chew noiselessly; to sop up juices with pieces of bread; and to avoid watching fellow guests dispatch their food. If the lady at your side "should raise an unmanageable portion to her mouth, you should cease all conversation with her, and look steadfastly into the opposite part of the room." [29]

The question of knife *versus* fork gained fresh urgency from the recent introduction of the French or silver fork in place of the steel variety. According to the social arbiters, both refinement and safety recommended the primacy of the fork, Mrs. Farrar alone dissenting. This Harvard professor's wife, insisting patriotically that "Americans have as good a right to their own fashions as the inhabitants of any other country," defended the practice of eating with a knife "provided you do it neatly, and do not put in large mouthfuls, or close your lips tight over the blade." [30] From the frequency of mention it was evidently not unusual for guests to break dishes, or even "to throw down a waiter loaded with splendid cut-glass." If such a mishap occurred, "you should not make an apology, or appear the least mortified, or indeed, take any notice whatever of the calamity." Otherwise the impression might arise that the host could ill afford the loss.[31]

When conversing, whether at the table or elsewhere, pains should be taken not to remind one's companions of their plebeian origins—that "you remember their living in a small house, or in a remote street." On the other hand, you mustn't yourself put on airs by boasting of "the fine things you have at home," for that might make people suspect "you were, not long ago, somebody's washerwoman, and cannot forget to be reminding everybody that you are not so now." [32] Another mark of the newly arrived was inconsiderate treatment of domestics. Though etiquette manuals granted that the yeasty republican spirit, fortified by the many other opportunities for employment, often rendered the servants themselves intractable, they placed the chief onus upon the mistresses who, unaccustomed to authority, used it tyrannically.[33]

In many respects women were conceded a larger measure

of freedom than the older dispensation had allowed. Since parents might unexpectedly lose their means, girls were urged to master some branch of knowledge or skill by which they could become self-supporting. The reading of fiction was no longer taboo, though the utmost discrimination was recommended. Ladies, if modestly attired, might also with full propriety take long journeys alone and even converse at times with respectful strangers.

Courtship, on the other hand, continued to be the only proper basis of companionship with the other sex. It was well for the man to take the initiative because custom so decreed, and in any event, "where there is a fair chance of every woman's being married, who wishes it, the more things are left to their natural course the better." Under the circumstances a girl was cautioned: "Accept not unnecessary assistance in putting on cloaks, shawls, over-shoes, or anything of the sort. . . . Read not out of the same book; let not your eagerness to see anything induce you to place your head close to another person's." Moreover, "the waltz is a dance of too loose a character, and unmarried ladies should refrain from it altogether." [34]

Wedlock, a visiting Frenchman thought, condemned a wife to "the life of a nun" except that it was "not taken ill that she have children, and even many of them." Though he somewhat embroidered the reality, the fact of woman's continuing submergence as a yokemate and mother sheds light on the unvarying advice of the manual writers not to contract a loveless union, even if the maiden's parents should insist. But seemingly only one mentor went so far as to suggest that a girl might sometimes be justified in marrying in defiance of her parents' desires.[35]

The unprecedented demand for dissertations on decorum in the generation before the Civil War shows how thoroughly the rising classes rejected the view: "I don't know what etiquette is, but I know what I like." Out of their need and wish came the behavior book in the modern sense of a code of arbitrary conventions framed for polite society. The regulations were avowedly designed for urban dwellers, with the drawing-rooms of Washington providing the model.[36] (New York's turn would come later.) How far the canons penetrated the countryside, and how far they affected all classes even in the cities, it would be difficult to say.

The important thing is that the preachments set up standards of deportment of which nearly everybody in one way or another became conscious. It was also significant that these standards were tacitly accepted as desirable not merely for the rich and the wellborn, but also for the rank and file.

Nor were the results inconsiderable. In the 1830's Tocqueville, judging from the vantage ground of French aristocracy, found American manners "neither so tutored nor so uniform" as in his own country, but "frequently more sincere." [37] Twenty years later, in 1857, Gurowski, a Polish nobleman's son, noted that the people still tended to neglect the "most minute details and rites of courtesy," but added, "good-breeding prevails, and hearty, intentional politeness marks their address and intercourse." The moral he drew was: "Democracy teaches self-respect to everybody, in respecting others." [38]

THE CULT OF ELEGANCE

AFTER THE CIVIL WAR SOCIAL AND ECONOMIC CONDITIONS FASHIONED A NEW MATRIX FOR AMERICAN MANNERS, ONE THAT endured with little change till the first war with Germany shattered the mold. Before the sectional contest most men had been content to strive for the comforts rather than the luxuries of life; large fortunes had been rare and unspectacular. But in the decades that followed, the worship of the Golden Calf came to engross all types of people, and as the careers of such persons as Jay Gould, John D. Rockefeller, Cornelius Vanderbilt, Andrew Carnegie, Henry H. Rogers, Philip D. Armour, Henry C. Frick, James J. Hill and Collis P. Huntington show, it was not unusual for the very poor to vault into the ranks of the fabulously rich.

The war itself spawned a brood of profiteers—government contractors and others who, because of the reputation some of them bore of cheating Uncle Sam with defective cloth for army uniforms, became known indiscriminately as the "shoddy aristocracy." According to the *Scientific American,* September 15, 1866, "There are more men in New York today whose annual incomes reach $100,000 than there were twenty-five years ago of those whose entire possessions amounted to as much." As a writer on social cultivation put it, "The war of 1861 swept away what little was left of that once important American fact—a grandfather. We began all over again." [1]

The biggest prizes fell to those who in the long peacetime years took advantage, by fair means or foul, of the virgin opportunities in manufacturing, mining, railroading, banking, stockjobbing, urban real estate, public utilities and the like. Incomes of $100,000 seemed like petty cash when, according to an economist in 1889, a hundred Americans averaged profits of $1,200,000 a year.[2] This was the age of copper and oil barons, steel kings, merchant princes, railroad magnates, Napoleons of finance. "The modern nobility," the Wall Street broker Henry Clews wrote solemnly, "springs from success in business," putting to shame the "English parchment nobility." [3] By 1902 the United States was credited with more than thirty-five hundred millionaires, and by 1916 the number had climbed to nearly thirteen thousand five hundred.[4]

The owners of these regal fortunes—or, more accurately, their wives—helped to set the social pace of the times. Just how the "gold rush" crashed the portals of exclusive society is only of incidental interest in this delineation of a nation's manners. It might perhaps be summarized in Mrs. William K. Vanderbilt's success in maneuvering Mrs. William Astor into attending her sumptuous fancy-dress ball on the night of March 26, 1883.[5] It may be viewed from another angle in William Dean Howells's account of how the women of the self-made Silas Lapham's family eagerly studied etiquette manuals in preparation for a dinner at the aristocratic Coreys.

It appears in still a different guise in the fervid exclamation of a poor Irish prospector on striking gold in Colorado, "Thank God, *now* my wife can be a lady!" [6]

Suffice it to say that, sooner or later, all but the crudest parvenus (and even some of them) scaled the heights and, once there, proceeded to show what dollars could do to destroy the older simplicities of society in favor of greater pretentiousness and conspicuous consumption. In a parody on Marx it might be said that they had nothing to lose but their change. "Is it possible," asked E. L. Godkin wryly, "that we are about to renew on this soil, at the end of the nineteenth century, the extravagances and follies of the later Roman Empire and of the age of Louis XIV?" [7] "The sham aristocracy indulge in mushroom-manners," agreed a specialist on etiquette.[8]

For the most part these manners were borrowed consciously, if sometimes with bizarre effect, from Europe, where a hereditary leisure class held the position which America's newly rich anguished to attain in their own country. As one contemporary wrote in justification, "We have imitated whatever we have considered wisest and pleasantest in the habits of the French, English, and other nations," though with particular preference for the French, whose observances were "less heavy and more graceful" than those of the English.[9] The Gallic influence appeared even in the language of the handbooks, for the writers seldom failed to give *ton* to their recommendations by calling them *au fait, recherché* or *de rigueur*. Transatlantic customs thus gained a repute that had been wanting since Washington's day.

While members of the middle class could not emulate Mrs. Vanderbilt's ball or afford to give a $10,000 dinner party at Delmonico's, they enviously followed the activities of the Four Hundred in the society columns, and since some of the mounting national wealth spilled over into their own pockets, they were better able than their class had ever been before to copy many of the ways of the smart set.[10] To be sure, special difficulties faced the South, where the Civil War and Reconstruction impoverished the landed proprietors, but even there the changed conditions cleared the way for the rise of a well-to-do business and financial class in the cities, and in time Southern manners came to approximate those of the North.[11] New York, as America's commercial capital, inevitably became also America's social capital, elbowing aside Washington, which had served as the court of last appeal for the preceding generation. Etiquette writers needed only to cite Manhattan's latest fashions in order to establish their right to speak with finality.

True, a certain amount of concern continued to be shown for those who needed to learn the mere rudiments of urban cultivation. As long as America should fall short of being Utopia, such a class would be in evidence. In the late nineteenth and early twentieth centuries its ranks were swelled by the mass immigration of peasants and workingmen from Southern and Eastern Europe. A further problem, though less stubborn, was presented by the increasing numbers of country folk who, accustomed to natural rather than artificial manners, crowded into the cities. For such backward groups one widely advocated solution was to teach the young idea how to shoot.

As the editor of *Scribner's Monthly* saw it, "The parents and teachers of the country can give us a polite people," but being skeptical of the effectiveness of the domestic influence, he placed the prime responsibility upon the schools.[12] Though this opinion was nearly as old as the first English settlements in the New World, the postwar generation seized on it with fresh gusto. Many of the newer states and territories of the Middle and Far West, following the example set earlier by the older commonwealths, now prescribed formal instruction in "morals and deportment," and publishers readily obliged by providing ample grist for the teacher's mill in the form of special handbooks.[13]

While magazine editors heartily seconded these efforts to indoctrinate the young, they devoted their principal endeavors to the broader task of raising the general average of adult behavior, addressing themselves to all who would heed, whether rich or poor. This task was no longer regarded as the sole obligation of women's journals, for in the decade or so following the Civil War such periodicals as the *Galaxy*, the *Round Table*, *Appletons' Journal*, the *Atlantic*, *Lippincott's* and *Putnam's* took up the burden.[14] Beginning in the 1890's, *Life* contributed indirectly to a knowledge of the usages of high society through Charles Dana Gibson's brilliant caricatures. Even the *Ohio Practical Farmer* campaigned for better manners, though it protested against the "observance of arbitrary rules laid down, perhaps, by a brainless fop," and saw no objection, for example, to eating pie with a knife.[15]

The chief responsibility, however, continued to be borne by the women's magazines, which could not have shed it if they had wished, thanks to the endless inquiries on points of etiquette from their readers. These letters, said the editor of the *American Queen,* poured in "from young ladies in the West and East; . . . from young men who are rising in the world . . . ; from elderly people to whom fortune has come late, but whose children begin to wish to know how to take their places in the gay world; from all parts of the country, in fact." [16] When Edward Bok secured "Ruth Ashmore" (Isabel A. Mallon) to conduct a department on social propriety and heartaches for the *Ladies' Home Journal,* her "Side Talks with Girls" brought her a hundred and fifty-eight thousand letters in sixteen years.[17]

The daily press was slower in discovering this avenue to reader interest, but as the newspapers steadily widened their scope to embrace feminine affairs, they dwelt increasingly on matters of good form as well as on personal problems. Then in 1896 "Dorothy Dix" (Mrs. Elizabeth M. Gilmer) revealed the true possibilities of this departure by launching her column of advice in the *New Orleans Picayune,* and two years later "Beatrice Fairfax" (originally Marie Manning) introduced the feature into the *New York Journal.*[18] Soon the number of such counselors became legion, and through syndication their views of proper conduct reached untold millions of people. They inaugurated an innovation in American journalism whose popularity has not yet shown signs of decline. Though they specialized on timely suggestions to the lovelorn, in the course of doing so they illuminated many other aspects of social usage.

As in earlier years, however, it was the etiquette book that constituted the bible of those who wished to be primed for all occasions. Not only were these volumes always on hand for reference, but they covered social contingencies for which there was no time to consult a distant editor. Some of the women's magazines recognized this fact by systematizing their precepts in such convenient manuals as *The Bazar Book of Decorum* (1870), of which Dr. Robert Tomes was the unacknowledged author; *The American Code of Manners* (1880), compiled from the *American Queen;* and *Social Life* (1889), taken from the *Delineator.* On her own, Mrs. John Sherwood of *Harper's Bazar* turned out a succession of handbooks under such titles as *Amenities of Home* (1881), *Manners and Social Usages* (1884) and *The Art of Entertaining* (1892).

Among others who lent their pens or names to such performances were Mrs. John A. Dahlgren, wife of the Civil War admiral; Maurice F. Egan, man of letters and diplomatist; Mrs. John A. Logan, widow of Blaine's running mate in the 1884 election; Rose E. Cleveland, sister of the man who triumphed over Blaine (and who kept her composure during the inauguration by conjugating a Greek verb); Mrs. Burton Harrison, descendant of the only colonial Virginia family with an undisputed place in the British peerage; Oliver B. Bunce, author and publisher, who hid his identity under the pseudonym "Censor"; Margaret E. Sangster, novelist and one-time editor of the *Bazar;* and Florence Howe Hall, biographer, suffragist and daughter of the revered Julia Ward Howe.

According to an incomplete list, new etiquette books for

grown-ups streamed from the press at the rate of five or six a year between 1870 and 1917, greatly surpassing even the record before the Civil War, and probably involving far larger editions, though for this latter conjecture data are lacking.[19] "People purchase them," thought one of the authors, "with an uneasy sense of shame, read them *sub rosa,* and keep them out of sight." [20] If so, it was not because of what the books contained, but because of the self-confessed need implied by buying them.

This avalanche swept aside practically all the older treatises. The new scribes assumed on the part of their readers a knowledge of those simple rules of republican deportment which the earlier writers had toiled to implant. Some, fearing lest the equalitarian spirit destroy all sense of the "relative duties of superior and subordinate," called for a sober second thought.[21] As etiquette authorities now saw their mission, it was to instill a more aristocratic style of behavior, one consonant with the improving fortunes of the middle class. To persons who flinched at the thought of greater formalism *Appletons' Journal* said, "Are not over-refinements better than under-refinements? Is it not better to carry punctiliousness a little too far than continually to be sinning against those minor morals on which the pleasure of intercourse so much depends?" The writer insisted with E. L. Godkin and others that mere amiability should not be mistaken for good breeding: "Training is necessary to repress and art to express." Even the austere Godkin conceded that the "social art" should rather be learned "from books, or by study, than not at all." [22]

Etiquette conceived of as art acquired an aura that had been lacking when it was viewed more prosaically as a species of unofficial law. With the maturing of American civilization people were coming to pay greater deference to cultural concerns, were growing increasingly sensitive to the fact that in the graces of living their own great country lagged behind the Old World. Nothing loath to profit by this inferiority feeling, many authors of social Baedekers upheld the new conception of etiquette by going in for such titles as *The Art of Pleasing, The Art of Good Manners, The Art of Good Behavior, The Art of Being Agreeable, The Art of Dining* and *The Art of Speech and Deportment.*

The emphasis on sophisticated manners led to exhaustive specifications of what to do in every conceivable situation: how high to lift one's skirt when crossing a street ("A lady should gracefully raise her dress a little above her ankle"); when and how to bow ("The head should be bent; a mere lowering of eye-lids, affected by some people, is rude"); how to shake hands (avoid either the "pump handle shake" or the "cold clammy hand" resembling a fish); how and when to write acceptances and regrets; how to make calls ("The formal call should not exceed fifteen minutes"); what to wear at morning functions, in the afternoon and at the ball or opera; and so on *ad infinitum.* Little wonder that one mentor proudly remarked that "not even a saint could, from his 'inner consciousness' alone, evolve a conception of the thousand and one social observances of modern fashionable life." [23]

Conversational ease was one hallmark of the *élite.* People

were advised: "Always think before you speak," and "Never emphasize a remark by a touch of the foot." "It would seem hardly necessary to remind any one of the undecorousness of sleeping in company, but it must be recollected that the obligation is equally urgent upon all not to put people to sleep." Greatly to be reprehended was the woman, so frequently met, whose mind was "bounded on the north by her servants, on the east by her children, on the south by her ailments, and on the west by her clothes." On the other hand, "only the half-educated" thought that "long words and high-sounding phrases are *distingué.*" This and other ways of showing off should be sternly repressed if one wished to avoid the *faux pas* of the lady who, being asked whether she had seen the Dardanelles while abroad, replied, "Oh, yes; we dined with them several times!"

As to appropriate topics for discussion, "there are always articles of virtu, photographs of foreign subjects, paintings, or statuary to be admired, and the conversation may gradually center on the Egyptian obelisk, or the Tower of London." In preparation for a social function it was well "to outline your subjects and fortify yourself by such study as you can make of them, or gain as much information as possible." [24]

To be sure, not every occasion called for learned talk. A model conversation at a dinner party might proceed as follows:

The gentleman may say, "We must be careful not to step on that elaborate train," referring to the costume of a lady preceding the pair.

"Yes, indeed, that would be a mishap. But trains are graceful in spite of their inconvenience."

Her companion must answer: "Oh! I admire them, of course. Only I have such a dread of stepping on them and bringing down the wrath of the fair wearer on my devoted head." . . .

Having seated themselves, and exchanged a few comments (of course flattering), on the table decorations, the lady, wishing to ascertain whether her companion was one of the silent diners-out, might say: "Some people do not care to eat and talk at the same time, but prefer to let what few comments they make come in between the courses."

"A man must be a dull fellow who cannot do both, with satisfaction to his neighbor if not to himself."

"Then I may talk to you without fear of interrupting your enjoyment of your dinner? But you speak as though it were easier to please your neighbor than yourself."

"Set down that speech to my gallantry."

And so on through the evening.[25]

For some years after 1865 personal elegance on the part of a gentleman required the adornment of whiskers. "There is nothing that so adds to native manliness as the full beard if carefully and neatly kept. . . . The person who invented razors libeled nature." The Civil War had been fought largely by generals who ambushed themselves behind beards, and every President from Grant on followed the same mode until Cleveland entered the White House in 1885 after defeating the bewhiskered Blaine. (Since then, it may be noted, all our chief executives have been beardless with a single exception, and he slipped into office without a majority of the popular votes!) Cleveland's clean-shaven jowls denoted a shift of taste that extended far beyond political circles. Before the end of his first term an authority on good form announced, "Beards have gone out of fashion," adding bluntly, "No one should wear a beard unless he have a preternaturally ugly mouth and chin." [26]

As the hairy face lost favor, so also did the frock coat. This full-skirted garment reaching almost to the knees had, as Godkin said, once been deemed to be the only attire in which "a serious-minded man, with a proper sense of his origin and destiny, and correct feelings about popular government, could make his appearance in a lady's parlor." Now it yielded, "though not without some tribulation," to the dress coat, which etiquette preceptors sanctioned as "the cosmopolitan evening dress, acknowledged everywhere from Indus to the pole."

The implications of the new attire were not always understood, however, and it proved necessary to inform wearers: "A gentleman in a dress-coat and a white tie feels as uncomfortable in the daylight as would a lady in low neck and short sleeves." [27] Yet the severity of full dress also came in for challenge when at the turn of the century the members of New York's exclusive Tuxedo country club adopted the English fashion of the tailless dinner jacket, which promptly became known as a tuxedo. This garb, however, was proper only at stag affairs or, at the most, at informal mixed dinner parties in the summer.[28]

The ancient prejudice against men's smoking in the presence of the other sex or "on a public promenade, where one is likely to meet ladies," still lingered, and one arbiter declared as late as 1891, "We think the prospects for the future happiness of that young girl are small, who will be seen in public with a gentleman who is smoking." President McKinley, anxious even about male users of the weed, refused to allow his picture to be taken with a cigar in his mouth, remarking to the photographer, "We must not let the young men of this country see their President smoking!" Nevertheless, increasing evidence in and out of manners books suggested that "modern notions on the tobacco question," even among women, were "growing lax." "Ladies no longer affect to be disgusted by the odor of tobacco, even at table," stated a writer in 1887, while another considered a cigar (though not a pipe) permissible "when by the seaside, or in the country, or in any but fashionable quarters, if your fair companion does not object."

That the fair companion herself might take up smoking was greeted as "a horror and a crying shame" by an etiquette author in 1898, who admitted, however, that "women, and women in America—in certain sets—do smoke." It was a habit recently introduced from Europe by a few brave souls who self-consciously puffed an occasional cigarette "in corners, when at clubs or races." [29] Most of the early twentieth-century manuals ignored the reprehensible practice, perhaps as the best way to banish it. When it became known that "Princess Alice," President Theodore Roosevelt's oldest daughter, sometimes indulged, the public was seized with consternation.

A more immediate danger to good breeding was the feminine love of display in costume and jewelry. "It is an indication that the growing wealth of the people is not accompanied by a corresponding refinement," reflected one expert on deportment, while another, sounding an ethical note, believed that women oftentimes assumed a "glamour of pomp" in order to dazzle people into forgetting that their "husbands have made immense sums of money in disreputable varieties of commerce." Still a third writer preferred to think that the evil lay not in the wealthy "being glorious in garb as are princesses and queens. They have a right so to be. But when those who can ill afford alpaca persist in arraying themselves in silk, because Mrs. So-and-So does it, the matter is a sad one." Notwithstanding this disapproval of excesses all etiquette treatises vindicated the right of woman not "to make herself a discordant object in this beautiful world of ours." If she spent hours polishing her silver, why should she not also spend time in making herself attractive? Let her remember, however, that the best cosmetics are diet, exercise, soap and water, not "loud perfumery," hair dye, powder and paint. "The way in which some women kalsomine themselves is frightful to see." [30]

Among the many new intricacies of social intercourse none perhaps occasioned more grief than the proper use of the calling card.

> Oh, what a tangled web we weave,
> When first we practise cards to leave!

Quite apart from such details as the correct size and typography was the difficult symbolism involved in bending the edges. Turning down the upper right-hand corner signified a personal visit; the upper left corner, congratulations; the lower right corner, adieu; the lower left corner, condolence; the entire left end, a call on the whole family. This practice, introduced from abroad shortly after the Civil War, commended itself to city dwellers who had little time or inclination for individual visits and yet did not wish to feel negligent of their social duties. As a result, a matron might have several hundred people on her list whom she hardly knew by sight. Despite its conveniences the custom was becoming *passé* by the 1890's. The sign language proved too great a tax on the human intelligence. "In consequence of the various interpretations liable to be given to the act," confessed an etiquette authority, "its disuse is a satisfaction to all persons concerned." [31]

"Nowhere has the growth of luxury in this country been more apparent," exulted a contemporary, "than in the pomp and circumstance which now accompanies modern dinners." In contrast to simpler times the guest found at his place "a bewildering number of glass goblets, wine and champagne glasses, several forks, knives, and spoons, and a majolica plate holding oysters on the half shell." From five to eighteen courses were not unusual at formal functions, and the agony was seldom ended short of two hours. Obviously "ease, *savoir-faire,* and good breeding" were "nowhere more indispensable than at the dinner-table, and the absence of them nowhere more apparent."

To allay the strain on both entertainer and entertained, service *à la Russe* became the rule. ("It is strange that the Russians, so lately redeemed from barbarism, have taught the world how to serve a dinner.") By the new mode the host neither carved nor served, all the food being made ready elsewhere and carried by servants to the guests, who were apprised by menus of the shape of things to come. Etiquette writers in applauding this practice did not fail to point out, "Both host and guest are relieved from every kind of responsibility. Dish after dish comes round, as if by magic; and nothing remains but to eat and be happy." Even the planning of the feast might be rendered painless, for by resorting to a professional caterer the host could "order a party as he orders his coat of a fashionable tailor." [32] What a boon for the socially inexperienced!

Though warnings against eating with a knife continued, it was assumed that the well-mannered would not offend. Grover Cleveland as presidential candidate in 1884 so deeply resented an opposition taunt that he mishandled the implement that, even after his election, he declined to shake hands with the editor responsible. The cult of the spoon, however, was colliding with a new one of the fork. "The true devotee of fashion," asserted a high priest of manners in 1887, "does not dare to use a spoon except to stir his tea or to eat his soup with, and meekly eats his ice-cream with a fork and pretends to like it." But, as time went on, some experts showed signs of relenting, one of them stating in 1898, "It is in order now to eat ice-cream and berries with a spoon, also puddings and sauces." Nevertheless, as late as 1910, social orthodoxy clung to the sterner dogma, informing the well-bred "never to use a knife or spoon when a fork will suffice." As for other fine points of dining, the guest was advised that "if by chance anything unpleasant is found in the food, such as a hair in the bread or a fly in the coffee, remove it without remark"; and if the guest himself erred by "tipping over a glass of red wine, breaking a dish, dropping a knife or fork," he should dismiss the incident with "a deprecatory look to the hostess and, perhaps, the briefest expression of regret." [33]

The ballroom presented its own special difficulties, and on these the handbooks lavished whole chapters without accomplishing much more, however, than making clear that the ordinary rules of courtesy applied with necessary modifications. It was new, of course, for the ball to be accepted by etiquette manuals as morally unobjectionable, and this fact seems all the more surprising in view of the steady encroachment of the relatively intimate round dances on the old-fashioned square dances. Probably the reason lay in the eagerness with which this generation, doggedly sophisticated, seized on social novelties involving glitter and display.

At any rate, as early as the 1870's authorities on behavior derided the idea that the ballroom was a "pitfall covered with flowers," or that there was anything "wrong in dancing." On the contrary, "a lady in society must, if she would not grow utterly weary in company, know how to dance. . . . It is one of the most healthful and elegant amusements, and cannot be too highly recommended." [34] To be sure, the waltz elicited the caution that "a gentleman never encircles the lady's waist until the dance begins, and drops his arms as soon as it ends," but even this mild reproof was omitted as the conviction grew that "there is impropriety in the suggestion of impropriety." In 1889 John Philip Sousa's tuneful composition, "The Washington Post," floated the two-step into popularity, providing the waltz with a close rival. Of the older dances only the German or cotillion survived. "The most fashionable dance of society," the cotillion was the grand climax of every well-conducted ball, a complex, colorful affair executed under a practiced leader and involving the frequent changing of partners and the presentation of expensive favors. By the eve of the first war with Germany, however, it too had given way to the waltz and two-step.[35]

For induction into the social world a maiden (but not a youth) had to endure a tutelage hitherto little known in the United States, but *de rigueur* in the best circles abroad. Allowed to be her natural self until seventeen or twenty, the young lady then made her *début* at an elaborate party where she was formally presented to her parents' friends and possible future suitors. Thereafter, if she and her parents were determinedly *au fait,* she entered a sort of servitude under the surveillance of a chaperon. She must not receive men in her home alone ("Compromising positions are easily fallen into, and a woman should be constantly on her guard"). She was not permitted to make formal calls alone, or go unchaperoned to dinners, receptions, balls, concerts or the theater. Even when betrothed, she could not attend a play with her *fiancé* or drive with him after dark in a closed carriage except in the presence of an older woman. The penalty for disobedience was harsh: "The woman who is in society at all must conform to its conventional laws, or lose caste in proportion to her defiance of these laws." [36]

To be sure, this effort to "fasten European social fetters upon our daughters of Freedom" met with resistance from young America. The etiquette guides found it constantly necessary to hammer away at the desirability of the practice. The chaperon, they pointed out, assumed responsibility for seeing that her unversed charge was properly clad for every occasion, saved her from countless social blunders and kept her from knowing the wrong people. In the large modern cities, where strangers were always coming in and transients were common, the "innate propriety of American women and the chivalrous nature of American men" no longer erected a sufficient shield against males who might be wolves in sheep's clothing. The presence of a chaperon, moreover, prevented any misunderstanding on the part of foreign sojourners. "A young Frenchman who visited America a few years ago formed the worst judgment of American women because he met one alone at an artist's studio. He misinterpreted the profoundly sacred and corrective influences of art." [37] After Henry James published *Daisy Miller* in 1879 his unfortunate heroine—an innocent abroad who affronted Old World conventions in associating with men—became a stock example of what American girls should not be and do. Unintended by the author, the story had an effect on American canons of behavior which students of James's literary influence have not taken into account.

Nevertheless the protagonists of the duenna fought an uphill battle. Young ladies as well as young men prided themselves upon their self-reliance and claimed the right to make their own decisions. As for the increasing numbers who were entering business and the professions, they could not understand why they should be under a guardian's feet at night after being on their own feet all day. Probably few were persuaded by the analogy to Cinderella who, it was said, toiled unattended in the dust and ashes, but required the oversight of the fairy godmother when she went to the ball. Even the manuals conceded that "with every year of a woman's life after twenty-five she becomes less the subject of chaperonage" as she leaves behind "the wild grace of a giddy girlhood." [38]

In small towns and rural communities none of the arguments for protective custody proved convincing, and in such places the custom failed to strike root.[39] In cities, on the other hand, it came to be considered "one of the elegances of life, one of the graces of the best society," even if not always observed in less polished sets. An authority on decorum, reviewing the improvement of metropolitan manners over a generation, felt warranted in saying early in the twentieth century, "Daisy Miller is almost an extinct species." [40]

Under the watchful eye of the chaperon courtship proved more difficult, but it was argued in compensation that the maiden's desirability, like that of fruit hung teasingly beyond reach, was correspondingly enhanced. All writers agreed that, as in bygone days, the actual wooing was an affair for the couple alone, with the admonition, however, that "marrying for a living is the hardest way a woman can take to get it."

"Proposals by women, while permissible," stated another authority, "are not customary." The parents' blessing, though every "manly man" should seek it with a full statement of his assets and prospects, was "merely a matter of form, as good parents obey their daughters." [41]

With the assumption of wifely responsibilities the young lady need no longer play second fiddle to her husband, but she could not escape another affliction of her mother's generation: the servant problem. Apart from sage preachments to both mistress and maid ("They were not foreordained from all eternity to be sworn enemies") and careful specifications as to the duties of various grades of servants, the social mentors did little to advance the solution of the question.[42] In the long run relief, if not solution, was to come from the spread of apartment living and the multiplication of labor-saving household gadgets, delicatessen stores, commercial laundries and bakeries.[43]

The two generations between the Civil War and the first war with Germany thus contrived a complicated structure of etiquette, sustained by the increase of national wealth and modeled upon the aristocratic usages of the Old World. Though not all members of the urban middle class conformed, and though country dwellers were doubtless still less affected, no one anywhere was left in doubt as to what the best society thought was proper. It behooved even rural youth to take heed, for many of them would eventually settle in the cities and the chances for success were better if "a person going from one place to the other, should be utterly undistinguishable from those about him." [44] Would the future see these standards gain universal acceptance, or would the adage *Autres temps, autres mœurs,* so often invoked by etiquette manuals to discredit older ways, operate in turn to undermine the elaborate edifice they had so painstakingly reared?

RELAX!

"THERE ARE SIGNS," DECLARED THE *CENTURY* MAGAZINE IN 1911, "THAT WE ARE IN THE PRELIMINARY STAGE OF AN ERA OF BETTER manners." [1] But the editor misread the portents. To the more discerning eye the signs pointed disturbingly in the opposite direction. Already the etiquette books had had to make concessions in such niceties of usage as men's evening dress and the ritualism of calling cards; the battle for chaperonage had never been quite won; and society's proudest achievement, the cotillion, was losing its glamour. Further changes clearly impended as city distances and the rush of life increasingly interfered with ceremonious intercourse, and as the exodus into the suburbs or into apartment houses limited the physical means for entertaining.

Moreover, the mere possession of money was no longer the exciting fact it had once been; indeed, the popular antagonism to great fortunes, symbolized by the Muckrakers, inclined the wealthy to eschew outward ostentation and show. Finally, women, the traditional custodians of polite deportment, were in their greater economic independence finding other interests far more absorbing than the social world. Even their growing addiction to outdoor sports infused into their bearing "something of the wild striding of the athletic field," and helped to diminish the touch-me-not quality which the etiquette writers had assiduously tried to nourish.[2]

The World War of 1917–1918 and the hectic decade that ensued completed the transition to a new set of social values. The postwar deterioration of public morals coincided with a laxer attitude toward private morals and manners, or so it seemed to those who revered the older canons. "Day by day the art of living withers and fades, leaving us to face existence, unadorned, in all its nakedness," wept a magazine contributor.[3] Though the struggle with Germany raised a fresh crop of American millionaires, they no longer wielded the scepter in society that their predecessors had, while the middle class, reveling in lush prosperity and openly defiant of what they considered outmoded "Victorian" conventions, made a fetish of freedom and self-expression.

Other factors also came into play. The "noble experiment" of prohibition, operating on the forbidden-fruit principle, spread the habit of drinking in unexpected directions.[4] The automobile, which mass-production methods had recently made cheap enough for anyone to own, encouraged a more informal companionship of the sexes, and the movie, popularizing Hollywood ideas of good form, further endangered inherited standards. The radio too did its part by acquainting the remotest rural outposts with the changing urban ways and ideas. Though the Great Depression sheared away most of the excrescences of behavior, by that time the old days were dead beyond recall.

Despite the social unruliness following the war, etiquette

books retained their hold on popular favor. In the years 1918–1929 sixty-eight different works (excluding revisions and juveniles) were published, according to a partial tabulation, and from 1930 to 1945 seventy-eight more came from the press—an over-all average of more than five a year, approximating the figure for the post-Civil War era.[5] Neither prosperity nor depression seemed much to vary the rate of production, and some of the treatises attained phenomenal sales.

The various versions of Lillian Eichler's *Book of Etiquette,* first issued in 1921, attracted over a million buyers by 1945, while Emily Post's *Etiquette, The Blue Book of Social Usage,* appearing in 1922, sold more than two thirds of a million copies of its successive editions by the same year.[6] From the early 1930's on, Mrs. Post further extended her influence by broadcasts and by a syndicated column which eventually appeared in a hundred and sixty dailies. Included among the host of other authors were Hallie Erminie Rives, Inez Haynes Irwin and Margaret Culkin Banning, all well known as novelists. *McCall's, Vogue* and the *Boston Cooking School Magazine* kept up the older tradition of women's journals by getting out their own manuals.

The continued popularity of these handbooks seems surprising at first. Doubtless it stemmed in part from the usual emergence of new classes from below, but it was probably due in far greater measure to the need many earnest souls felt for a steadying hand in a period of bewildering flux in social conventions. Puzzled and disturbed by the négligé state of manners, they disliked being thought old fogies and hence losing touch with their children; yet, on the other hand, they wanted to make certain that youth was not headed straight for perdition. Some, to be sure, itched to learn whether they too, despite their different upbringing, might not adopt the freer, franker ways of the rising generation. By the same token, the etiquette preceptors faced a perplexing choice. Either they could stand like granite against change—and risk the loss of sales—or they could make judicious concessions to the new.

The course of Emily Post is instructive. Born to wealth and position, formally launched into society in 1892 (four men often being required to bear her cotillion favors to her carriage), widely traveled abroad, then left to support her children after the failure of her marriage to a wellborn New York banker, she composed her initial manual on politeness in the firm desire to preserve the punctilious standards that had constituted her own heritage. But within five years she suffered a change of heart, for letters from some fifty thousand readers acquainted her with outlying America and convinced her that she was defending a lost cause. The revision of 1927 was pithily characterized by one reviewer as "putting a kick in etiquette to pacify flaming youth." On her part Mrs. Post now serenely, if tardily, announced that each generation had a right to interpret social law to suit itself. The chapter in the original volume on "Chaperons and Other Conventions" became "The Vanishing Chaperon and Other New Conventions." "As for the matter of smoking by women and girls," the author, no addict herself, declared in a magazine article, "it must be countenanced, for there is scarcely a fashionable home today in which the girls and women of the family do not smoke." In subsequent editions and writings she minimized still further small points of form, declaring that "no rule of etiquette is of less importance than which fork we use." [7]

Yet Emily Post did not go as fast or as far in yielding to the new anarchy as many of her rivals. Despite the resolve to march abreast of the times her pages never quite concealed her wistful longing for the decorous past. By contrast, Lillian Eichler, who entered the field while an employee in a New York advertising agency, saw good from the start in the revolution in manners. Elaborating her position in the edition of 1924, she flayed "the stilted formalities of another age," declaring that the simpler ways were "sane and wholesome, creating a sense of ease and comfort in social intercourse rather than a feeling of stiff formality and restraint." Furthermore, she emphasized, "The new etiquette does not 'lay down the law.' It offers suggestions that are based upon modern tendencies and that are subject to changing conditions and circumstances." The reader was even warned: "What is regarded as highly ill bred now may be acceptable before you have finished reading this book." [8]

Evidently with some other authority in mind than Miss Eichler, the youthful compilers of *Mrs. Grundy Is Dead* a few years later expressed impatience at being told "what should be done rather than what actually is done," and they based their own treatise on the results of a questionnaire sent to college boys and girls all over the land.[9] The disclosures, however, proved less shocking than the book's title

—which is some measure of the extent to which modern ideas of behavior had become legal tender.

The fact is that, with whatever reluctance, most professional votaries of etiquette adopted the coloration of the post-war age, sanctioning usages that would have caused their predecessors to turn in their graves. From her former high position the chaperon now became the vermiform appendix of American society, surviving only as "a clawless creature without any force in her peck," who was tolerated at week-end parties, formal dances and late gatherings in a man's apartment. "The girl of to-day . . . has her own good sense and knows how to meet the 'jazz age' halfway, without destroying any of the old family standards." Though Mrs. Post continued to hold out against a girl using her own latchkey at night, even she admitted it was no longer a social taboo. In the opinion of another arbiter, "The girl who defies the laws of health by habitual late hours is more apt to draw down a criticism of her brains than of her morals." [10]

Young people in their new freedom might "be together constantly without being engaged or having the slightest intention of being engaged. There is no reason why a young woman may not have men friends just as she has women friends." However, "since men enjoy the belief that they are the pursuers, let them do the pursuing," otherwise she may "run after a man who runs faster!" As to how far into the dawn she should stay out motoring, the majority of college girls consulted replied, "It all depends upon the man." "Necking" and "petting," though regarded by Emily Post as quite outside the subject of etiquette, came in for due attention from her colleagues "because many young men now take a good-night kiss as a matter of course." How should the well-bred miss respond?

"Even if his kiss would be acceptable let him make the first move," admonished one mentor, who added that, if on the contrary the girl felt disinclined, she should refuse "in such a way that he won't be hurt or get the impression that you're an old-fashioned prude." Another expert contended that a girl would "not lose many dates by not petting," for her escort did it "partly because it is the most obvious way of enjoying himself and partly because he thinks the girl expects it." By allowing "familiarities other than kissing," all agreed that the young lady merely cheapened herself: "the reputation of being a 'hot number' is anything but complimentary." [11]

As another mark of emancipation, women need no more be secretive about how they enhanced their beauty: "Gone are the days of the surreptitious rouge-pot." [12] "Applying lipstick in public," said a second authority, herself an impeccable socialite, "is supposed to outrage good taste," but "I would rather see a girl dabbing powder on her nose or putting lipstick on her lips than going shiny-faced and wan-lipped." [13] The feminine habit of smoking now excited only such comments as: "It is entirely permissible for a girl not to smoke if she doesn't wish to, provided she is not ostentatious about it"; and "When you smoke be sensible about it, particularly if he's furnishing the cigarettes, and never, never smoke on the street" (though "many women do," sighed another author, "even those who know better"). The rule of moderation applied also to women's drinking: "Take only the amount you're positive you can handle and stop the minute any doubt assails you." [14]

Similarly, the use of slang, once forbidden to the well-bred of either sex, was sanctioned as sometimes adding "piquancy to our talk"; even "'swell' and 'sweetie pie' are correct in certain moods of conversation." In all moods of conversation, it was stated, "there is scarcely a subject left which is considered too delicate to discuss in the drawing-room." As for men swearing before ladies, one college youth adjured his fellows, "Try not to," while another observed, "If they say 'damn,' so do I, when useful." [15]

"In nothing has there been greater change," noted an etiquette book, "than in the manner in which we entertain." "Today," agreed another, "informal parties are the rule and not the exception. For one thing, they represent the trend of the times; for another, they are more friendly," and, she added not irrelevantly, "They are also less trouble." [16] One of the most popular varieties was the cocktail party. Though cocktails had occasionally been served earlier in the century as an appetizer for dinner, the practice was "one more honored in the breach than in the observance," according to an arbiter in 1911. Late afternoon gatherings with mixed drinks and relishes as the bait were a postwar innovation, and it now was a matter of course that "every dinner, informal or otherwise, should be preceded by a cocktail." [17]

With entertaining taking the path of least resistance the ordeal of "coming out" threatened to pass into disuse. Unlike the "starry-eyed debutante" of yesteryear, we are told, "the modern girl is 'half-out' before she is sixteen, and at eighteen she is bored with teas and receptions and does not care one whit whether her mother's friends like her or not." If the parents proved obdurate, however, there were ways of cushioning the blow, for the debut could take the form of anything from a ball or afternoon tea to the "mere sending out of the mother's visiting card with the daughter's name engraved below her own." [18]

Dinner parties suffered a similar eclipse. "The dinner table that groaned under the load of ten or twelve courses has vanished," announced one instructor in manners, and "the successful hostess is not she who can display the richest silver, but she who can make her guests feel comfortable and happy." With simplified repasts menu cards also took wing, and men might attend all but the most formal affairs in a tuxedo (though "the nickname 'tux' is never heard among smart people"). The fastidious still donned full dress for a box at the opera, an evening wedding or a fashionable ball. "If you can afford only one evening suit," advised a social mentor, "buy the dinner jacket rather than the tails because it is used more frequently." [19]

As with other ceremonious functions, balls in the grand manner entered a decline, being unable to stand competition with dancing parties of "lesser formality and greater gayety." "Some of our austere grand-dames would feel righteously indignant if they were suddenly brought back to the ballroom and forced to witness some of the modern innovations," wrote a social preceptor, who for her own part approved of the "crash of jazz" and the "shoulder-shaking, oscillating dancing of today, . . . joyous, unrestrained, a little mad." If she stretched the truth a bit in stating that "the new etiquette welcomes it good-naturedly," the fact remains that neither silence on the subject nor cautious opposition succeeded in reversing the tide.[20]

Taken as a whole, the postwar customs struck both the self-appointed mentors and the practitioners as restoring simplicity, common sense, spontaneity, to American deportment after a prolonged affliction of pretense and repression. "Paradoxical as it may seem," declared one of the sponsors, "this liberty of behavior requires more real breeding than ever. You must have an innate sense of the fitness of things, and sure feeling for the correct time and place." It was the spirit, not the appearance, that counted, manner rather than manners; or, as another writer put it, "The elegance of today is not rococo, but functional." [21]

Oddly enough, the result was to flavor urban sophistication with a naturalness that smacked of bucolic folkways. The uninhibited association of the sexes proved hardest for the older generation to accept, but when they saw instance after instance of the wild young thing maturing into responsible womanhood, they came to believe that the age was not more wicked than others—it just failed to pull down the shades.

The relaxed attitude toward regimented politeness made etiquette in the older sense fair game for humorists. When Will Rogers read the first and starchiest of Emily Post's treatises, he concluded that the author had set about her task because "somebody must have seen me out in public." Professing fascination at her description of a butler's proper attire, he rejoiced in the fact that, having learned that this functionary should never wear braid on his trousers, he would henceforth be able to distinguish a butler from a gentleman, even though "more than likely the Butler is the Gentleman of the two." [22]

About the same time Donald Ogden Stewart, fresh from writing his successful *Parody Outline of History*, directed mocking shafts against *Perfect Behavior*, a volume which *Harper's Bazar* unblushingly copyrighted. Starting with the definition: "The perfect gentleman is he who never unintentionally causes pain," Stewart ran the whole gamut of formalized etiquette.[23] Of conduct on the street he earnestly observed, "It is not *au fait* for gentlemen or ladies wearing evening dress to 'catch on behind' passing ice wagons, trucks, etc." With like urgency he warned against such "good-natured fun" at a dinner party as "pulling the hostess' chair out from under her, or gleefully kicking the shins of your neighbor under the table and shouting 'Guess who?' " Cleverness in society he thought could be carried too far: "slow and sure" was the better rule. "No hostess of today will, I am sure, ever issue a second invitation to a young man who has attempted to enliven her evening by balancing, on his nose, a knife, a radish, a plate of soup and a lighted candle." [24] The American public, once daunted by rules uttered with equal solemnity, rocked with laughter.

In this climate of freedom, however, a new branch of manners came to full bloom. Long ago Chesterfield had taught that politeness paid; and as the growth of industry and trade after the Civil War opened up countless new careers for men and women, expositors of good form often recurred to the theme. But not until the twentieth century began to draw out its length did the subject become one for full and separate treatment. The motive may have been to try to offset business ethics with business etiquette, or to show enterprising merchants how to realize upon a neglected asset. "Bad manners are going out of American business," proclaimed the author of one of the volumes. "Common sense did it. Courtesy increases business, so we eliminate boorishness with the same sweeping efficiency with which we scrap old machinery." [25] A further aim of the writers was to coach women employees in relations which lay outside their ordinary social experience. Nella Braddy's *Book of Business Etiquette,* published in 1922, was followed within two years by Ida W. Parker's *Office Etiquette for Business Women,* and encouraged by their success, rivals began to throng the market.[26]

Department stores, banks and other large concerns, cashing in on the idea, provided systematic instruction by means of manuals, bulletins, conference groups and classroom exercises, drilling young people in etiquette "with the same thoroughness that they drill them in making out sales slips." The neophytes learned that it was improper to say "O. K." and "All righty"; that they must never dispute with a shopper even when he was wrong ("It is useless to win an argument and lose a customer"); and that they should always speak kindly to children when accompanied by a parent. The teaching of these and similar dogmas was justified on the ground that "artificial good manners are preferable to natural bad manners."[27] And so, by a strange juxtaposition of circumstances, stereotyped politeness, having been ejected from the drawing-room and the dance floor, found an unforeseen asylum in the marts of trade.

THE BALANCE SHEET

"IMMEDIATELY AFTER THE WORLD WAR," WROTE AN AUTHORITY ON SOCIAL USAGES, "FORMALITY WAS PUSHED ASIDE WITH A barbaric shout." [1] What impress would the later and greater world conflict make? The answer, of course, lies in the future,[2] but while the war was still going on, American manners were subjected to an unaccustomed test.

Earlier in the century, when the nation was embarked on a policy of colonial aggrandizement, it viewed etiquette as an exportable commodity, and in the case of the Philippines it strove through the schools to indoctrinate the natives with Yankee ideas of decorum. "No Filipino boy or girl," complacently reported an American in 1913, "can go through the primary grades without acquiring a complete education in the use of knife, fork, and spoon." [3] But the same nation, having subsequently repented of its flier in imperialism and subscribed to the Four Freedoms and the principles of the Atlantic Charter, had to recognize—officially at least—the right of every people to its own social customs. In any case, military prudence so required, for if the millions of American soldiers and sailors imposed their manners as well as their might upon the far-flung countries where they were obliged to train or fight, the result might be resentment and friction instead of tolerance or friendly co-operation.

Hence the United States government issued a series of "pocket guides" for servicemen, explaining the national characteristics and usages of the particular peoples, with warnings against Star-Spangled ways that might give needless offense.[4] The recurring refrain was: "Every American soldier is an unofficial ambassador of good will." In Britain, the ambassador was told, "It isn't a good idea to say 'bloody' in mixed company—it is one of their worst swear words." Before entering a Moslem home in North Africa he should "call out to the women to cover their faces," and at dinner sit on the floor and eat with his fingers out of the same bowl as his companions. In Egypt, the directions continued, "Take off your shoes before entering a room," "Don't offer a Moslem alcohol or pork in any form," and "Ignore Egyptian women completely."

A special admonition regarding India read: "Treat every cow with respect," and for similar reasons the GI in Burma was enjoined not to injure large trees since "some of the Burmese venerate these objects." The Chinese, he must remember, "don't like to be slapped on the back" and, what was probably more to the point, "the Chinese like reserve with their women."

It doubtless afforded real relief to learn that the French colony of New Caledonia was "comparatively free from religious taboos which make it difficult for the visitor to get along in other countries," though it was less welcome that "in some families it would not be considered proper for a girl to go out on a date unless accompanied by her parents or a chaperon." Only in the British commonwealths in the Pacific could the serviceman feel genuinely at home. "There are no striking differences between the United States and New Zealand in ordinary social life," he was assured, and he "should find it easy to get along," while he was probably startled to discover that "the Australians, especially the girls, are a bit surprised at the politeness of American soldiers."

This enforced contact with alien cultures, while testing the adaptability of American manners, also demonstrated the diversity of codes of behavior that coexisted in the world and, at least for the thoughtful, helped to clarify the interrelationship of a people's social usages and their national system of life. It had the effect of unfolding on a flat surface of space what the history of American courtesy revealed longitudinally in segments of time. As a dynamic society the American people had adopted and discarded a succession of codes, ranging all the way from the primitive approximations of English standards in the colonial period through the emerging stages of national freedom, democracy and sudden wealth in the nineteenth century to the take-it-or-leave-it attitude of the aging twentieth century.

At first, politeness was so closely identified with morality as to be scarcely distinguishable. It was then usual to define manners as "minor morals." Lord Chesterfield's writings, however, helped to drive a wedge between the two, a process which reached completion when the middle classes came to the top, intent on aping the ways of those whom they had formerly deemed to be of finer clay. Etiquette now managed to disentangle itself from ethics, taking on its modern meaning of a generalized pattern of behavior designed to lubricate social intercourse. Courtesy so defined was likened to law, and its prescriptions were set down in a multiplicity of popular manuals written by Americans for Americans, though not without an eye on foreign models. With the rising standard of comfort after the Civil War, art became the new justification of etiquette, with elegance as the means of accomplishment. Morals, law, art—these catchwords, each so potent in its own day and generation, gave way in turn before the reign of informality following the World War of 1917–1918. Had the latest comers deigned to defend their ways, they would probably have invoked some such term as pragmatism.

United States history affords few better instances of the interworkings of continuity and change. At any given moment the code of behavior was like a palimpsest, showing tracings of older writings under the new. Oncoming generations, insisting on innovations suitable for their times, commonly took for granted certain inherited axioms of conduct. While the forces for change were generated largely by American conditions, the earliest canons of courtesy harked back to the Middle Ages, and throughout United States history the example of the Old World, notably England and France, wielded a fluctuating influence.

Obviously there were always discrepancies between preaching and practice. The rules of etiquette were calculated, as an astronomer would say, for the meridian of the city, and even there it was "good society" that paid principal heed. Nevertheless the little candle threw its beams afar, and as time toned down the differences between urban social classes and between country and town as well, something like a nation-wide consensus of manners came about. The authors of manuals characteristically offered a counsel of perfection, but they scored chiefly in fostering tendencies already in the making. Like the man in the familiar story, they led the procession by following it. When, as happened at rare intervals, they forgot their restricted role, the public cashiered them and substituted other leaders in their place.

Despite the constant winnowing of manners generation after generation, certain niceties of usage never commanded the universal assent of the authorities or received final adjudication. At the table, for example, must the hostess be served first or last? Should a guest start eating without waiting for his fellows? Should the diner manipulate his fork with his left or right hand? And how, oh how, should one eat corn on the cob?

The coming of the elevator after the Civil War precipitated the debate over whether gentlemen should remove their hats in the presence of ladies, the answer depending on whether the handbook regarded the conveyance as a room or a public passageway. Much earlier, with the introduction of horse-drawn omnibuses on city streets in the 1820's, began the controversy as to whether a man should give up his seat to a strange woman. It involved also the correlative question of how the recipient should acknowledge the favor. On these two points of propriety the authorities generally expected the utmost politeness from both parties, but the actual practice became increasingly remiss. If a current tale is to be believed, a man on a motorbus rose and surrendered his place to a lady —and she fainted. When she came to, she thanked him— and he fainted.

Has politeness ever had more than a decorative value in American life? Clearly many eminent persons have thought so, for men like Cotton Mather, Benjamin Franklin and George Washington gave the subject time and thought, and Ralph Waldo Emerson stands forth as perhaps the ablest philosopher of manners. "Their first service," he observes, "is very low,—when they are minor morals; but 't is the beginning of civility,—to make us, I mean, endurable to each other . . . . to get people out of the quadruped state; to get them washed, clothed, and set up on end." Once these initial lessons are learned, "the power of manners is incessant . . . . Men take each other's measure, when they meet for the first time,—and every time they meet. . . . It is not what talents or genius a man has, but how he is to his talents, that constitutes friendship and character." Though moral qualities rule the world, "at short distances the senses are despotic," and he adds, "Defect in manners is usually the defect of fine perceptions." Outer forms must not be scorned, for human society, "being in its nature a convention, loves what is conventional, or what belongs to coming together." Even from an esthetic point of view manners deserve respect as "a rich varnish with which the routine of life is washed and its details adorned. If they are superficial, so are the dew drops which give such a depth to the morning meadows." In brief, manners "recommend, prepare, and draw people together; . . . manners make the fortune of the ambitious youth; . . .

for the most part, his manners marry him; and, for the most part, he marries manners; . . . what high lessons and inspiring tokens of character they convey, . . . what relations to convenience, power and beauty." [5]

To some people fixed social rules have appeared a system of hypocrisy; to some, heartless formality; to others, an invidious expression of class distinctions; and to still others, an instrument of torture. The purpose of etiquette, remarks a modern cynic, is to enable one to seem a gentleman without being one. Its purpose, says another, is to make guests feel at home when they wish they were. But in letting fly at the abuses rather than the uses of etiquette, such objections largely miss the mark. "If I am polite to you," writes the author of a widely used manual, "it is not necessarily because I love you, but because I want to make my intercourse with the world as pleasant as possible, both for myself and the people I meet." In the words of a Frenchman, the precepts are intended to "make one seem externally what one ought to be internally." [6] Even the outward motions imply a certain kindliness and consideration for others. Nor, except for the tyro, do the commandments complicate social life nearly as much as they simplify it: "It is a wonderful comfort to have islands of certainty to swim to when one plunges out from self into society. . . . The more we put recurring movements into form, the more mind we have left for spontaneous living that is refreshing and pleasant." [7] Etiquette, once fitted to the lock, thus becomes a key to freedom.

Politeness, however, has a significance beyond the domain of personal relations. As an etiquette writer has put the case,

"Neither the history of mankind in general, nor the history of any one nation in particular, can be duly understood and appreciated without a much fuller knowledge of the rise and progress of manners and customs than has hitherto been deemed necessary either by historians or students." [8] Manners not only make the man but, to a surprising degree, also a people. Few traits more quickly reveal a person's nationality than the habitual way he acts; by this sign he instantly subscribes himself an American, a Frenchman, an Italian.

Within a nation, differences in social demeanor tend to nourish misunderstanding and friction. It was no mere coincidence that the rift between North and South occasioning the Civil War corresponded with a similar rift in the manners of the two sections. "What Thucydides said of the Greeks at the time of the Peloponnesian War applies to us at present," wrote Francis Lieber in 1860 from firsthand knowledge of both sets of disputants. " 'The Greeks,' he said, 'did not understand each other any longer, though they spoke the same language; words received a different meaning in different parts.' " [9] Conversely, it was no mere coincidence that the farmers' movements of later times declined in rudeness and stridency as the manners of East and West grew more alike.

If foreign immigration had transplanted to the United States the traditional social customs of the homelands, the process of assimilation would have been greatly retarded. Yet, from the standpoint of courtesy, Americans of older stock might have profited from contact with the kindly and obliging deportment of many of the aliens. As a commentator remarked, however, "One who knows the immigrant as working-man or servant knows that one of the notable facts concerning him is the sudden shedding of politeness in the first six months after setting foot on Ellis Island." [10] The stranger at the gates was one against many, and adjustment to the unfamiliar was more a necessity than a choice. Within the family circle he might try to preserve the immemorial usages, but as his children absorbed American ways from their playfellows and schoolmates, the home too had to succumb, or else abdicate its influence in their lives.

While the national yardstick of manners presented difficulties for foreign newcomers, it facilitated both the geographic and social mobility of the older population. From first to last the people were in incessant motion, shifting about from one region to another and, increasingly as time went on, from country to city. Next to a common language, they carried no better letter of introduction than their adherence to common precepts of courtesy. By the same token, they or their children looked forward to moving upward in the social scale, and here again nothing stood them in better stead than their knowledge of what "good society" expected. It is easy to deride the copying of rules of politeness by those who had nothing to do with setting them, but in America the willingness to imitate has in the long run had the effect of lessening artificial class distinctions.

In a still broader context good manners play a role in international affairs. "In the field of world policy," the late President Roosevelt declared in his first inaugural, "I would dedicate this nation to the policy of the good neighbor—the neighbor who resolutely respects himself and, because he does so, respects the rights of others." [11] Traditional diplomacy had regarded the letter rather than the spirit of etiquette. Needless to say, this investment in neighborly courtesy has yielded swift dividends in better relations between the United States and the sister republics of the New World. Even with the promise of banishing war afforded by the United Nations, rulers will spare mankind much anxiety, and perhaps bloodshed, if they remember that a soft answer turneth away wrath and that consideration for the rights and sensibilities of other peoples will almost certainly elicit like consideration in return.

ACKNOWLEDGMENTS

I AM DEEPLY INDEBTED to my secretary, Elizabeth F. Hoxie, for assistance in research and for help in putting the manuscript in shape for the printer. My wife, Elizabeth Bancroft Schlesinger, aided me by her steady interest and wise counsel. To Zoltán Haraszti, head of the Rare Book Department of the Boston Public Library, I am grateful for permission to revise for book publication the series of essays which appeared originally in *More Books* (January-April, 1946). I wish further to thank the following publishers for the privilege of quoting from the books named:

D. APPLETON-CENTURY COMPANY, INC.

Doris Webster and Mary A. Hopkins, *Mrs. Grundy Is Dead* (copyright 1930).

DELL PUBLISHING COMPANY, INC.

Ella Riddle, ed., *Modern Manners* (published 1939).

DOUBLEDAY, DORAN AND COMPANY, INC.

Lillian Eichler, *Book of Etiquette* (copyright 1921 by Doubleday & Company, Inc.) and *New Book of Etiquette* (copyright 1924 by Doubleday & Company, Inc.); Mary A. Hopkins, *Profits from Courtesy* (copyright 1937, reprinted by permission of Doubleday & Company, Inc.); and Donald Ogden Stewart, *Perfect Behavior* (copyright 1922, reprinted by permission of Doubleday & Company, Inc.).

ACKNOWLEDGMENTS

GREENBERG: PUBLISHER

Grace Harriman, *Book of Etiquette* (copyright 1942).

ALFRED A. KNOPF, INC.

Alice L. Moats, *No Nice Girl Swears* (copyright 1933).

J. B. LIPPINCOTT COMPANY

Margery Wilson, *The Pocket Book of Etiquette* (published originally as *The New Etiquette: the Modern Code of Social Behavior,* copyright 1937 by Margery Wilson).

A. M. S.

BIBLIOGRAPHY AND NOTES

A ROW OF STUDIES and bibliographies affords information about the English and Continental background of colonial manners. Of particular use are Gertrude E. Noyes, comp., *Bibliography of Courtesy and Conduct Books in Seventeenth-Century England* (New Haven, 1937); V. B. Heltzel, comp., *A Check List of Courtesy Books in the Newberry Library* (Chicago, 1942), which closes with the year 1774; A. S. Palmer, *The Ideal of a Gentleman* (London, 1908); Ruth Kelso, *The Doctrine of the English Gentleman in the Sixteenth Century* (Urbana, 1929); and J. E. Brown, *Gentlefolk in the Making* (Philadelphia, 1935), treating the period 1531–1774.

The subject of American manners has received relatively little attention. Dixon Wecter devotes an interesting chapter in *The Saga of American Society* (New York, 1937) to "The Book of Etiquette," largely from the standpoint of the social climber. E. H. Cady has written an unpublished study, "The Concept of the Gentleman in Representative American Writers," which is abstracted in the University of Wisconsin's *Summaries of Doctoral Dissertations*, VIII (1942–1943), 193–195. Occasional light is shed on colonial usages in L. B. Wright, *The First Gentlemen of Virginia* (San Marino, 1940); Julia C. Spruill, *Women's Life and Work in the Southern Colonies* (Chapel Hill, 1938); Mary S. Benson, *Women in Eighteenth-Century America* (New York, 1935); and Alice Morse Earle, *Child Life in Colonial Days* (New York, 1899), and other books from her pen. Nothing of equal relevance has been done for later periods, though the theme is touched on in Meade Minnigerode, *The Fabulous Forties* (New

York, 1924), and C. J. Furness, ed., *The Genteel Female* (New York, 1931), and in some of the volumes of A. M. Schlesinger and D. R. Fox, eds., *A History of American Life* (New York, 1927–1944).

None of these writings obviates the necessity of reading the etiquette books themselves. Unfortunately no comprehensive bibliography of them has been compiled, though Mrs. Vernon L. Bobbitt of New York City is engaged in preparing one. A special phase of etiquette, only incidentally noticed in the present study, has been better served by H. B. Weiss, *American Letter-Writers, 1698–1943* (first published by the New York Public Library in its *Bulletin* and then in 1945 as a booklet), which contains a "preliminary check list" of these manuals on the art of polite correspondence.

Practically every European traveler from earliest times commented on the state of American manners, but these appraisals, though often helpful, must be used with caution. The tartest critics, invariably Englishmen, were disqualified by their own ill breeding. As William Cobbett said, they expected their transatlantic cousins to be servile, not civil. The friendliest observers, on the other hand, were likely to have visited only in select circles, or to have allowed their enthusiasm for democracy to mellow their judgment. In the notes that follow will be found detailed references to the materials upon which the present account is based.

INTRODUCTION

[1] Anon., *The American Code of Manners* (New York, 1880), 11.

CHAPTER I. FIRST LESSONS

[1] The main facts are presented in Alice M. Earle, *Curious Punishments of Bygone Days* (Chicago, 1896), and Julia C. Spruill, *Women's Life and Work in the Southern Colonies* (Chapel Hill, 1938), chap. xv.

[2] W. H. Whitmore, ed., *The Colonial Laws of Massachusetts. Reprinted from the Edition of 1672, with the Supplements through 1686* (Boston, 1887), 206.

[3] Alice M. Earle, *Home Life in Colonial Days* (New York, 1898), 282–285, and W. B. Weeden, *Economic and Social History of New England, 1620–1789* (Boston, 1890), I, 226–228, 286–290.

[4] Benjamin Franklin, *Poor Richard's Almanac* (B. E. Smith, ed., New York, 1898), *passim,* and Nathaniel Ames, father and son, *Essays, Humor, and Poems* (Sam Briggs, ed., Cleveland, 1891), 251, 377.

[5] Bessie L. Pierce, *Public Opinion and the Teaching of History* (New York, 1926), 3–4.

[6] R. W. G. Vail, "Moody's *School of Good Manners*: a Study in American Colonial Etiquette," *Studies in the History of Culture, the Disciplines of the Humanities* (Menasha, 1942), 261–271, gives excerpts and traces the bibliographical lineage. A revised edition, sponsored by the Massachusetts Sunday School Society, appeared as late as 1846.

[7] An edition of 1837 altered the examples to "Father, Mother, Pa, Ma, Sir, &c."

[8] Vail, "Moody's *School of Good Manners*," 267, suggests the first explanation, but Charles Moore, editor of *George Washington's Rules of Civility and Decent Behaviour* (Boston, 1926), pp. x–xiv, 23–65, makes out a stronger case for the second. Alice M. Earle, *Child Life in Colonial Days* (New York, 1899), 219, unconvincingly attributes the Moody compilation to the same intermediate English treatise (Francis Hawkins's *Youths Behaviour, or Decency in Conversation amongst Men*) as that from which Moore believes young Washington drew.

[9] Washington's "Rules" should be compared with the Pennsylvania German schoolmaster Christopher Dock's "A Hundred Necessary Rules of Conduct for Children" (1764), first published in German in the *Geistliches Magazien* (Germantown), part i, no. 40, and reproduced for modern readers in his *Life and Works* (M. G. Brumbaugh, ed., Philadelphia, 1908), 167–174, 202–213. Dock's formulation, designed for his Mennonite coreligionists, covers a wider range of behavior and upholds more exacting standards. Interestingly enough, Washington's "Rules" were frequently reprinted in nineteenth-century etiquette manuals and even as late as 1904. Since the same faults did not then call for correction, it may be supposed that these later writers wished to bask in the reflected glory of the youth who became the Father of his country.

[10] L. B. Wright, "The Purposeful Reading of Our Colonial Ancestors," *ELH, a Journal of English Literary History,* IV (1936–1937), 100–101, and S. E. Morison, *The Puritan Pronaos* (New York, 1936), 131.

[11] Mary N. Stanard, *Colonial Virginia* (Philadelphia, 1917), 271. L. B. Wright, *The First Gentlemen of Virginia* (San Marino, 1940), is the authoritative treatment of that subject.

[12] J. C. Fitzgerald, *George Washington Himself* (Indianapolis, 1933), 149–150. A modern edition of Peacham's work, with an introduction by G. S. Gordon, was published by the Oxford University Press in 1907.

[13] These and other guides are described in Spruill, *Women's Life and Work in the Southern Colonies*, particularly chap. x, from which the present summary is largely derived.

[14] J. P. Brissot de Warville, as quoted by Dixon Wecter, *The Saga of American Society* (New York, 1937), 162.

CHAPTER II. PROGRESS IN THE NORTHERN PORTS

[1] When the English evangelist George Whitefield ran across this book on his trip through New England in 1740, he recommended it to all women, and a new edition was promptly forthcoming in Boston. For information regarding this and some other behavior guides used in the North, see Mary S. Benson, *Women in Eighteenth-Century America* (New York, 1935), 105–106, and *passim*.

[2] This volume was manifestly more than a mere money-making venture, for as early as 1733 Franklin had contrived a plan for "arriving at moral perfection" in his own life. He expected eventually to mature his views in a volume to be called *The Art of Virtue,* but his many other activities prevented. See his *Autobiography* (John Bigelow, ed., New York, n. d.), 147–165.

[3] Benjamin Franklin, *Writings* (A. H. Smyth, ed., New York, 1905–1907), III, 435.

[4] Apparently Richard Lingard's *A Letter of Advice to a Young Gentleman* (London, 1670), was the first to bear an American imprint, being republished in New York in 1696. See F. C. Erb's introduction to the modern edition of this work (New York, 1907). It was not, however, until some years later that the practice became common.

[5] According to the preface of *The Complete Letter-Writer* (Salem, 1797), "Business, duty, amusement, affection, courtship, friendship, and a

multitude of other affairs that may require a letter, are here made the subject of ours; so that, on most occasions no person can be at a loss for a pattern to direct him."

[6] Sometimes a single volume would contain selections from a variety of authorities. The most successful examples, both originally British compilations, were John Hamilton Moore's *The Young Gentleman and Lady's Monitor*, thirteen American reprints, 1787–1800, and anon., *The Lady's Pocket Library*, three, 1792–1797. Publication data are derived from Charles Evans, comp., *American Bibliography* (New York, 1941–1942), II–XII; Joseph Sabin and others, comps., *A Dictionary of Books Relating to America* (New York, 1868–1936); and S. L. Gulick, Jr., comp., "A Chesterfield Bibliography to 1800," Bibliographical Society of America, *Papers*, XXIX (1935).

[7] John Gregory, *A Father's Legacy to His Daughters* (Albany, 1821), 34–35.

[8] John Bennet, *Letters to a Young Lady* (Philadelphia ed., 1818), 110–111, 155, 157, 174.

[9] "Now, supposing a woman to have sense and taste," he remarked, "she will not find many men to whom she can possibly be supposed to bear any considerable share of esteem." Gregory, *A Father's Legacy*, 77–78.

[10] Bennet, *Letters*, 277.

[11] For the quotations in this and the preceding paragraph, see Philip Dormer Stanhope, Earl of Chesterfield, *Letters to His Son* (Boston and Newburyport, 1779), I, 144, 262–263, 393, 398; II, 15, 82, 528.

[12] Benson, *Women in Eighteenth-Century America*, 142; John Adams, Samuel Adams, James Warren and others, *Warren-Adams Letters* (Boston, 1917–1925), II, 129. For other American blasts, see Donald Fraser, *The Columbian Monitor* (New York, 1794), 90–91; the references cited in H. R. Brown, *The Sentimental Novel in America, 1789–1860* (Durham, 1940), 45, *n.* 76; and H. T. Tuckerman, "Lord Chesterfield," *Godey's Lady's Book*, XLIV (1852), 7–12.

[13] He went on: "All he has produced would immediately have perished with the other *frothy* bubbles of the day. . . . Society should *burn* his books." Bennet, *Letters*, 120, 217. For a full-length British indictment, speedily reprinted in America, see Thomas Hunter, *Reflections Critical and Moral on the Letters of the Late Earl of Chesterfield* (2d ed., London, 1777; 3d ed., Boston, 1780). Hunter condemned Chesterfield's "new invented distinction between morals and manners" and declared the work should be

entitled "*An entire Code of Hyprocrisy and Dissimulation.*" London ed., 77–78, 92.

[14] Apparently these were all reprints of abridgments originating in England. So great did Chesterfield's renown become in America that the translator of Abbé de Bellegarde's *Politeness of Manners and Behaviour* (Boston, 1821) knew no better way of gaining popular favor for the Frenchman's work than by saying the famous Earl had recommended the author to his son. Though it is true that Chesterfield had his pious moments, one still can't help wondering at his endorsing a treatise which began with the statement: "Politeness is a summary of all the moral virtues."

[15] Enos Hitchcock, *Memoirs of the Bloomsgrove Family* (Boston, 1790), I, 16–17; anon., "Comparison between Certain French and American Customs," *American Museum,* IV (1788), 121–122. Among other things, the latter writer commended the French for using individual glasses instead of "one vessel" when drinking people's healths, and for withdrawing from a company "without saying a word" instead of taking ceremonious leave.

[16] This volume (Philadelphia, 1827) also contained supplementary material, including "Ten Precepts" by Lord Burleigh and a short "Chapter Addressed to Americans." The latter (200–201) pointed out that good form in England tabooed certain practices common in the United States, such as spitting promiscuously, chewing tobacco, and "lolling back, balanced, upon the two hind legs of a chair."

CHAPTER III. REPUBLICAN ETIQUETTE

[1] The scornful phrase is quoted in a letter of Salmon P. Chase, April 20, 1829, in the *Ohio Archaeological and Historical Quarterly*, XXVIII (1919), 152.

[2] Anon., *How to Behave* (New York, 1856), 124.

[3] Catharine M. Sedgwick, *Morals of Manners* (New York, 1846), 61.

[4] A. M. Schlesinger, Jr., *The Age of Jackson* (Boston, 1945), 38*n*., 99.

[5] Quoted in Wecter, *Saga of American Society,* 35, from an article originally appearing in the Muscogee *Herald* in 1856.

[6] The quotation is from Sarah J. Hale, *Manners; or, Happy Homes and Good Society* (Boston, 1866), 142.

[7] Pierce, *Public Opinion and the Teaching of History,* 4–5*n*., 6–7.

[8] Alonzo Potter and G. B. Emerson, *The School and the Schoolmaster*

(New York, 1842), 176–177, 343–357; Charles Northend, *The Teacher and the Parents* (2d ed., Boston, 1853), 32–35, 55–57, 303–305.

[9] See, for example, Albert Picket, *The Juvenile Expositor* (New York, 1827), 191–196; William Sullivan, *The Political Class Book* (new ed., Boston, 1831), 143–148; S. G. Goodrich, *The Third Reader* (6th ed., Boston, 1841), 59–64, 117.

[10] Sara P. Willis [Parton], *The Life and Beauties of Fanny Fern* (New York, 1855), 284. See also her similar "Advice to Ladies" in *Fern Leaves from Fanny's Port Folio* (Auburn, 1853), 317–319, a work which sold 80,000 copies.

[11] For some reviews and notices of these works, see *Godey's Lady's Book*, XIV (1837), 47, 285; XVI (1838), 167–169, 225–228, 245–248; XVIII (1839), 192, 239, 285–286; XX (1840), 95; XXI (1841), 94; XXII (1841), 48; XXVI (1843), 59, 295–296; XXVIII (1844), 55, 200; XXX (1845), 143; XXXI (1845), 130; XXXV (1847), 156, 332; XL (1850), 356; XLIV (1852), 165, 167, 230; L (1855), 277; LII (1856), 182, 563; LIII (1856), 85, 564; LIV (1857), 280, 470; LX (1860), 471; LXII (1861), 179, 190; LXIX (1864), 176.

[12] R. W. Emerson, "Culture," in *Works* (Boston, 1883–1887), VI, 138.

[13] Review of Margaret Coxe, *The Young Lady's Companion* (Columbus, 1839), in *Godey's Lady's Book*, XIX (1839), 286.

[14] G. W. Hervey, *The Principles of Courtesy* (New York, 1852), p. iii. This indictment was quite too severe, though *Godey's Lady's Book*, XVIII (1839), 286, accused a recently published manual of reflecting the influence of "the old and heartless philosophy of Chesterfield."

[15] W. A. Alcott, *The Young Man's Guide* (rev. ed., Boston, 1844), 367–368. Miss Sedgwick in *Morals of Manners*, 43, said, "We hardly know whether it belongs to morals or manners, to offer the best seats at table to your elders, and to the females of your family."

[16] T. S. Arthur, *Advice to Young Men* (Boston, 1847), 70–71, and *Advice to Young Women* (Boston, 1847), 5–6.

[17] "The most thorough emetic I know of," Fanny wrote, "is in the shape of 'Guide to Young Wives,' and kindred books." Sara P. Willis [Parton], *Fresh Leaves* (New York, 1857), 210.

[18] Hale, *Manners*, 80.

[19] Catharine M. Sedgwick, *Means and Ends* (Boston, 1839), 15–16, 150.

[20] The quotations are from anon., *The Perfect Gentleman* (New York, 1860), 7–8; the preface of anon., *How to Behave*; and N. P. Willis, *Hurry-graphs* (Auburn, 1851), 300, 326. Margaret C. Conkling ("Henry Lunettes"), *The American Gentleman's Guide to Politeness and Fashion* (New York, 1857), 330, cautioned that "Rudeness and Republicanism" should not be considered "synonymous terms."

[21] The author of *The Perfect Gentleman*, 6–7, makes much of this point.

[22] For the rising-class phenomenon in England, consult C. W. Day ("Count Alfred D'Orsay"), *Etiquette* (New York, 1843), 3–4, and anon., *The Habits of Good Society* (New York, 1865), 24–26. For a brief recent discussion, see Lytton Strachey, *Portraits in Miniature and Other Essays* (New York, 1931), 118–119.

[23] Anon. ("A Gentleman"), *The Laws of Etiquette* (Philadelphia, 1836), 89.

[24] Anon., *Perfect Gentleman*, 200.

[25] Conkling, *American Gentleman's Guide*, 26.

[26] Anon., *How to Behave*, 18; Emily Thornwell, *The Lady's Guide to Perfect Gentility* (New York, 1856), 14; anon., *Perfect Gentleman*, 208.

[27] Eliza Leslie, *The Behaviour Book* (Philadelphia, 1859), 15.

[28] Elizabeth F. Bayle-Mouillard ("Mme. Celnart"), *The Gentleman and Lady's Book of Politeness and Propriety of Deportment* (Philadelphia, 1852), 83. This translation of a French work was reprinted many times.

[29] Anon., *Laws of Etiquette*, 151.

[30] Eliza W. Farrar (who used the pseudonym "A Lady" in the first printing), *The Young Lady's Friend* (Boston, 1836), 346–347. The revised edition (New York, 1873) by Clara J. Moore ("Mrs. H. O. Ward") deleted this heretical advice. A letter from Mrs. Farrar to her publisher, dated June 4, 1837, and preserved in the Boston Public Library, notes that certain passages in the original edition of her book offended the "fastidiousness of Boston readers," but the only one she specifies concerned instructions to nurses on how to treat the "evacuations" of patients (page 69). This she asked him to omit in future printings.

[31] Anon., *Laws of Etiquette*, 204–205.

[32] Leslie, *Behaviour Book*, 188; anon., *Perfect Gentleman*, 204, 205–206.

[33] The substitution of Irish and German servants for the older native "help" was another factor in the situation. On the "servile war," see Lydia H. Sigourney, *Letters to Young Ladies* (Hartford, 1833), 30–31; Conkling,

American Gentleman's Guide, 102–103; Farrar, *Young Lady's Friend,* chap. xi; and Harriet Beecher Stowe's "House and Home" (1864), pieces in the *Atlantic Monthly,* reprinted in *Household Papers and Stories* (Boston, 1896), 43, 99, 141–145. W. A. Alcott, pointing out in *The Young Wife* (Boston, 1837), 153–157, 166, that, unlike former times, people "in middling and even low circumstances" employed domestics, added, "The system of keeping servants in our families seems to me highly anti-republican."

[34] Farrar, *Young Lady's Friend,* 288–289, 293; Bayle-Mouillard, *Gentleman and Lady's Book,* 187.

[35] G. W. Pierson, *Tocqueville and Beaumont in America* (New York, 1938), 144; anon., *How to Behave,* 114.

[36] See, for example, the anonymous *Etiquette at Washington, together with the Customs Adopted by Polite Society in the Other Cities of the United States* (Baltimore, 1849; 3d ed., 1857). Of Washington, A. G. de Gurowski, *America and Europe* (New York, 1857), 406, said, "Men coming from all parts of the republic, independent and equal to each other in their public character, give and preserve to society the broad republican features and space wherein every one moves freely and finds his absolute or at least his relative appreciation."

[37] Alexis de Tocqueville, *Democracy in America* (Henry Reeve, tr., New York, 1900), II, 229.

[38] Gurowski, *America and Europe,* 375–376.

CHAPTER IV. THE CULT OF ELEGANCE

[1] Mary E. W. (Mrs. John) Sherwood, *Manners and Social Usages* (New York, 1884), 6.

[2] T. G. Shearman, "The Owners of the United States," *Forum,* VIII (1889–1890), 262–273.

[3] Matthew Josephson, *The Robber Barons* (New York, 1934), 315.

[4] Guernsey Camp, Jr., and others, *The New England Situation* (Chicago, 1927), 23–25.

[5] Wecter, *Saga of American Society,* 332–339.

[6] *Ibid.,* 316.

[7] E. L. Godkin, *Problems of Modern Democracy* (New York, 1896), 328.

[8] Clara S. J. Moore ("Mrs. H. O. Ward"), *Sensible Etiquette of the Best Society* (10th rev. ed., Philadelphia, 1878), 144.

[9] [Abby B. Longstreet], *Social Etiquette of New York* (New York, 1878), 12.

[10] Between 1870 and 1900 the national wealth quadrupled (rising from $30,400,000,000 to $126,700,000,000), and it doubled again by 1914 (reaching $254,200,000,000). R. R. Doane, *The Measurement of American Wealth* (New York, 1933), 10–11. Discussing the situation in the early 1890's, C. B. Spahr, *An Essay on the Present Distribution of Wealth in the United States* (New York, 1896), 129, concluded that "the general distribution of incomes in the United States is wider and better than in most countries of western Europe."

[11] W. F. Tillett, "Southern Womanhood as Affected by the War," *Century,* XLIII (1891–1892), 9–16, emphasized particularly the passing of the patrician ideal of the "nobility of helplessness in women."

[12] J. G. Holland, *Every-Day Topics* (New York, 1882), 356–357. In like manner the author of "Table-Talk" in *Appletons' Journal,* V, 686 (June 10, 1871), believed that "the essential coarseness and rudeness, that are the consequence of vulgar homes, may in some measure be qualified by the discipline of the school-room." One of the few etiquette books specifically designed for rural migrants to the cities was Mrs. Sara B. Maxwell, *Manners and Customs of To-day* (Des Moines, 1890). Immigrant arrivals had to get along as best they could, the single known exception being the *Guide for Newly Coming Women,* published by the Japanese Association of America (founded in 1908), which was distributed among Japanese women on shipboard while crossing the Pacific. It explained American manners, modes of living and attire and laid down rules of etiquette for both public and private occasions. See "Japanese Immigration," *House Report,* 66 Congress, 2 session (1920), 643.

[13] Besides the newer commonwealths of Minnesota, North and South Dakota, Arizona, Idaho and Utah, which acted between 1878 and 1896, West Virginia (1863) and Florida (1881) also passed such legislation. Pierce, *Public Opinion and the Teaching of History,* 15–21 and footnotes. Among the manuals designed to meet the need were J. W. Phelps, *Good Behavior* (2d ed., Brattleboro, 1876); Susan C. Power, *Behaving; or, Papers on Children's Etiquette* (Boston, 1877); anon., *Points of Etiquette* (New York, 1879); Elizabeth S. Kirkland, *Speech and Manners for Home and School* (Chicago, 1884); Edith E. Wiggin, *Lessons on Manners for School and Home Use* (Boston, 1884); Julia M. Dewey, *How to Teach Manners in the School-Room* (New York, 1888), and *Lessons on Man-*

ners (New York, 1899); and P. A. Barnett, *Little Book of Health and Courtesy* (New York, 1905). See also Margaret S. McNaught, "Training in Courtesy: Suggestions for Teaching Good Manners in Elementary Schools," U. S. Bureau of Education, *Bulletin,* LIV (1917), 1–42. Charles W. Eliot, "Democracy and Manners," *Century,* LXXXIII (1911), 173–178, summarized the results of an inquiry into the teaching of manners in 740 public schools, and from this sampling concluded, "There can be no doubt that the great majority of American public schools are actively contributing today to the diffusion and development of good manners among the people." Some years later Ruth Strang reported encouragingly on the "Knowledge of Social Usage in Junior and Senior High Schools" in *School and Society,* XXXIV (1931), 709–712.

[14] F. L. Mott, *A History of American Magazines,* III (Cambridge, 1938), 307–308, 376–377, 459.

[15] Department of Agriculture, *Farmers in a Changing World* (*Yearbook of Agriculture for 1940*), 160–161.

[16] Anon., *The American Code of Manners* (New York, 1880), p. i. For a similar statement by an editor of *Harper's Bazar,* see Sherwood, *Manners and Social Usages,* 7–8.

[17] Edward Bok, *The Americanization of Edward Bok* (New York, 1922), 169–171.

[18] Jacqueline McCullough, "'Always an Angle,'" *Editor and Publisher,* LXXIX, 60 (March 9, 1946); Marie Manning (Gasch), *Ladies Now and Then* (New York, 1944), 32–49, 103–128; F. L. Mott, *American Journalism* (New York, 1941), 599.

[19] This enumeration, omitting reprints, revisions and children's guides, shows 46 issued in the 1870's, 51 in the 1880's, 43 in the 1890's and 65 in the years 1900–1917.

[20] Anon., *Good Manners* (Philadelphia, 1870), p. iii.

[21] Catherine E. Beecher and Harriet Beecher Stowe, *The American Woman's Home* (New York, 1869), 198–199.

[22] "Table-Talk," *Appletons' Journal,* V (1871), 595; Godkin, *Problems of Modern Democracy,* 323. There were, of course, dissenters to Godkin's view of the etiquette work. Thus a writer in the *Atlantic,* XXVI (1870), 122, reviewing [Robert Tomes], *The Bazar Book of Decorum* (New York, 1870), smugly avowed that "all the behavior-books that ever were written" would not keep people from "betraying their unfashionable origin."

[23] The quotations are from anon., *Decorum* (New York, 1877), 122; Mrs. John A. Logan and others, *The Home Manual* (Boston, 1899), 22; Mrs. M. L. Rayne, *Gems of Deportment and Hints of Etiquette* (Detroit, 1880), 82; anon., *The Manners That Win* (Minneapolis, 1880), 82; anon., *Good Manners,* p. iv.

[24] For the quotations in this and the preceding paragraph, see anon., *Good Manners,* 35; Rayne, *Gems of Deportment,* 40, 164; Tomes, *Bazar Book of Decorum,* 121; Florence (Mrs. Burton) Kingsland, *The Book of Good Manners* (Garden City, 1901), 363; Lillie d'A. Bergh and others, *Correct Social Usage* (New York, 1906), I, 54; Mrs. Sara B. Maxwell, *Manners and Customs of Today* (Des Moines, 1890), 194.

[25] Logan and others, *Home Manual,* 47–48, which also gives examples of small talk at an afternoon tea, a musicale, a reception and a ball.

[26] For the two quotations on beards, see anon., *Decorum,* 320, and Lydia E. White, *Success in Society* (Boston, 1888), 97–98.

[27] For quotations in this and the preceding paragraph, see E. L. Godkin, *Reflections and Comments* (New York, 1895), 217; Moore, *Sensible Etiquette,* 256–257.

[28] W. C. Green, *A Dictionary of Etiquette* (New York, 1904), 138; Eleanor B. Clapp, *Social Usage and Etiquette* (New York, 1910), 149–150.

[29] The quotations in this and the preceding paragraph are from Ingersoll Lockwood, *The P. G. or, Perfect Gentleman* (New York, 1887), 113, 189; Annie R. White, *Polite Society at Home and Abroad* (Chicago, 1891), 221; William Allen White, *Autobiography* (New York, 1946), 332–333; R. A. Wells, *Manners, Culture and Dress of the Best American Society* (Springfield, Mass., 1890), 139; anon. ("A Woman of Fashion"), *Etiquette for Americans* (Chicago, 1898), 179–180.

[30] Florence Hartley, *The Ladies' Book of Etiquette* (rev. ed., Boston, 1873), 298; [Abby B. Longstreet], *Social Etiquette of New York* (New York, 1878), 175–176; Moore, *Sensible Etiquette,* 252–253; Rayne, *Gems of Deportment,* 273–275, 282; anon., *American Code of Manners,* 36.

[31] Florence H. Hall, *Social Customs* (New York, 1887), 33; White, *Success in Society,* 178; Rose E. Cleveland, ed., *The Social Mirror* (St. Louis, 1888), 122; Margaret O. Forbes-Lindsay ("Mrs. Charles Harcourt"), *Good Form for Women* (Philadelphia, 1907), 44–46; Maud C. Cooke, *Social Etiquette* (Boston, 1896), 60.

[32] For quotations in this and the preceding paragraph, see Cleveland,

Social Mirror, 148; Sherwood, *Manners and Social Usages,* 177, 182, 187; anon., *Good Manners,* 103, 110, 125; anon., *American Code of Manners,* 71, 79; anon., *Manners That Win,* 125.

[33] W. C. Hudson, *Random Recollections of an Old Political Reporter* (New York, 1911), 237–238; Hall, *Social Customs,* 87; anon., *Etiquette for Americans,* 92; Clapp, *Social Usage and Etiquette,* 230; Young, *Our Deportment,* 127; anon., *American Code of Manners,* 362; Forbes-Lindsay, *Good Form for Women,* 151.

[34] Hartley, *Ladies' Book,* 198, 202. See also Tomes, *Bazar Book of Decorum,* 89. That the approval was not universal, however, is shown by the fact that as late as 1904 Margaret E. Sangster, despite the title of her book, omitted all mention of dancing from her *Good Manners for All Occasions* (New York), a work sponsored by the *Christian Herald.*

[35] Anon., *Manners That Win,* 355; Kingsland, *Book of Good Manners,* 171–173; Clapp, *Social Usage and Etiquette,* 88; Ellin C. (Mrs. Frank) Learned, *The Etiquette of New York To-day* (New York, 1906), 50–51; Hall, *Social Customs* (rev. ed., Boston, 1911), 178.

[36] Anon., *Manners That Win,* 44–45; Green, *Dictionary of Etiquette,* 288; M. F. Egan, *A Gentleman* (New York, 1893), 58–59; Hall, *Social Customs* (1887 ed.), 179; Sherwood, *Manners and Social Usages,* 99, 146–150; Agnes H. Morton, *Etiquette* (Philadelphia, 1892), 133–134.

[37] Tomes, *Bazar Book of Decorum,* 117; Sherwood, *Manners and Social Usages,* 145–146, 150.

[38] Morton, *Etiquette,* 132–134; Sherwood, *Manners and Social Usages,* 153.

[39] For the rural resistance, see Morton, *Etiquette,* 126–128; Sangster, *Good Manners for All Occasions,* 82; Learned, *Etiquette of New York To-day,* 286; also James Bryce, *The American Commonwealth* (2-vol. ed., London, 1888), II, 590.

[40] Kingsland, *Book of Good Manners,* 193; Sangster, *Good Manners for All Occasions,* 81.

[41] Kingsland, *Book of Good Manners,* 194, 204–205; Harriet Beecher Stowe, *Household Papers and Stories* (Boston, 1896), 233; Green, *Dictionary of Etiquette,* 217; Sangster, *Good Manners for All Occasions,* 98.

[42] Mary V. H. Terhune ("Marion Harland") and Virginia Van de Water, *Everyday Etiquette* (Indianapolis, 1905), 300.

[43] From 1910 to 1920, for example, the number of delicatessens grew three times as fast as the population; between 1914 and 1924 the output

of bakeries rose by sixty per cent, and in the same decade the use of commercial laundries increased by fifty-seven per cent. F. L. Allen, *Only Yesterday* (New York, 1931), 96.

[44] Maxwell, *Manners and Customs,* 50–51, 366.

CHAPTER V. RELAX!

[1] *Century,* LXXXIII (1911), 310.

[2] Anon., "Futurist Manners," *Atlantic Monthly,* CXII (1913), 422.

[3] Elizabeth Robins Pennell, "Our Democracy of Bad Manners," *Forum,* LXXII (1925), 512.

[4] "We can't suppress an ironical snicker," said Alice L. Moats, *No Nice Girl Swears* (New York, 1933), 171, "that all they [the prohibitionists] succeeded in doing was transporting women from the drawing-room into the speakeasy."

[5] In addition, at least thirty-five courtesy books for children were issued between 1918 and 1945. The continued interest in school instruction in politeness is indicated by such treatises as E. Hawkes, *Social Training as a Curriculum Problem* (New Brunswick, N. J., 1927), and W. E. McVey, *Minimum Essentials in Manners and Right Conduct for Schools* (Columbus, Ohio, 1929).

[6] Alice P. Hackett, *Fifty Years of Best Sellers, 1895–1945* (New York, 1945), 98, 106.

[7] Margaret C. Harriman, "Dear Emily Post," *Saturday Evening Post,* CCIX (May 15, 1937), 18–19, 52, 57; anon., "Emily Post," *Current Biography for 1941* (New York, 1941), 681–683; anon., "Emily Post," *Pathfinder,* Sept. 4, 1937, 16–17; anon., "Putting a Kick in Etiquette to Pacify Flaming Youth," *Literary Digest,* XCVI (Feb. 4, 1928), 56–59; Emily (Mrs. Price) Post, *Etiquette* (rev. ed., New York, 1934), p. xx, and "Any Fork Will Do," *Collier's,* LXXXIII (April 20, 1929), 21.

[8] Lillian Eichler (Mrs. T. M. Watson), *The New Book of Etiquette* (Garden City, 1924), I, 41–42; II, 34, 36. Miss Eichler, a cub copywriter just out of high school, became an etiquette author as the result of her success in disposing of several thousand copies of Emily Holt's outmoded *Everyman's Encyclopædia of Etiquette* (New York, 1901). As part of her campaign she invented the device: "What's Wrong in This Picture?" (See her *Etiquette Problems in Pictures,* Oyster Bay, 1922.) When droves of dissatisfied customers returned the books, Nelson Doubleday, the publisher, prevailed upon Miss Eichler herself to write an up-to-date work

on the subject, which she did in two months after office hours. Only eighteen at the time, she had no difficulty in sympathizing with rebellious youth. For her story, see W. E. Berchtold, "Men Who Sell You," *New Outlook,* CLXV (1935), 56, and Sidney Carroll, "Inside New York," *Ken,* III (March 9, 1939), 82–84.

[9] Doris Webster and Mary A. Hopkins, eds., *Mrs. Grundy Is Dead* (New York, 1930), 3 and *passim.* Two later manuals, somewhat similarly inspired, were *Manners Make Men; a Practical and Sparkling Manual of Modern Etiquette Written by University Men* (Lawrence, 1939), edited by H. B. Powers and J. W. Putnam of the University of Kansas, and *Lady Lore; a Swingtime Handbook for Girls* (Lawrence, 1939), edited by J. W. Putnam alone.

[10] Webster and Hopkins, *Mrs. Grundy Is Dead,* 63; Eichler, *New Book of Etiquette* (1924 ed.), II, 29; Post, *Etiquette* (1934 ed.), 290; Margery Wilson, *The Pocket Book of Etiquette* (New York, 1941; originally published as *The New Etiquette: the Modern Code of Social Behavior,* copyright 1937 by Margery Wilson, here quoted by permission of J. B. Lippincott Company), 17.

[11] For references in this and the preceding paragraph, see Eichler, *New Book of Etiquette* (1924 ed.), II, 37; Ella Riddle, ed., *Modern Manners* (New York, 1939), 61, 64–65; Webster and Hopkins, *Mrs. Grundy Is Dead,* 68; Post, *Etiquette* (1934 ed.), 296–297; Wilson, *Pocket Book of Etiquette,* 40. In the college poll reported in *Mrs. Grundy Is Dead,* 39, a majority of the men said that nice girls petted and that it was all right for them to do so.

[12] Moats, *No Nice Girl Swears,* 6.

[13] Grace (Mrs. Oliver) Harriman, *Book of Etiquette* (New York, 1942), 64–65. The author, the wife of a New York banker, is a cousin of the late E. H. Harriman and a sister-in-law of Mrs. W. K. Vanderbilt, Sr.

[14] Webster and Hopkins, *Mrs. Grundy Is Dead,* 93; Riddle, *Modern Manners,* 63; Harriman, *Book of Etiquette,* 28.

[15] Eichler, *New Book of Etiquette* (1924 ed.), I, 227; Harriman, *Book of Etiquette,* 83; Moats, *No Nice Girl Swears,* 7; Webster and Hopkins, *Mrs. Grundy Is Dead,* 36.

[16] Wilson, *Pocket Book of Etiquette* (originally published as *The New Etiquette: the Modern Code of Social Behavior,* copyright 1937 by Margery Wilson, here quoted by permission of J. B. Lippincott Company), 184; Harriman, *Book of Etiquette,* 111.

[17] Hall, *Social Customs* (1911 ed.), 107; Wilson, *Pocket Book of*

Etiquette, 191, 208–209, 243; Harriman, *Book of Etiquette,* 114, 124, 133, 353.

[18] Harriman, *Book of Etiquette,* 186; Eichler, *New Book of Etiquette* (1924 ed.), II, 29; Post, *Etiquette* (1922 ed.), 276.

[19] Eichler, *New Book of Etiquette,* II, 95–96; Wilson, *Pocket Book of Etiquette,* 88, 90; Harriman, *Book of Etiquette,* 512–513.

[20] Eichler, *Book of Etiquette* (1921 ed), II, 99, 101, 105, and *New Book of Etiquette,* (1924 ed.), II, 170–171.

[21] Moats, *No Nice Girl Swears,* 4; Eichler, *New Book of Etiquette* (1924 ed.), I, 24; Wilson, *Pocket Book of Etiquette* (originally published as *The New Etiquette: the Modern Code of Social Behavior,* copyright 1937 by Margery Wilson, here quoted by permission of J. B. Lippincott Company), 127.

[22] "Etiquette, as Lassoed by Will Rogers," *Literary Digest,* LXXIX (Oct. 6, 1923), 46, 50.

[23] This "old proverb," as Stewart called it, originated in Cardinal Newman's characterization of a gentleman as "one who never inflicts pain," which Oscar Wilde cynically amended by adding the word "unintentionally." Earlier in the century Charles Wayland Towne had anticipated Stewart with a heavy-handed volume entitled *Eediotic Etiquette* (New York, 1906). His notion of humor is indicated by the injunction: "Don't propose to a girl at a Horse Show. You are apt to get 'neigh' for an answer."

[24] D. O. Stewart, *Perfect Behavior* (New York, 1922), 71, 213–215.

[25] Mary A. Hopkins (Mrs. E. H. Jessup), *Profits from Courtesy* (Garden City, 1937), 1.

[26] Among the later handbooks were Elizabeth G. McGibbon, *Manners in Business* (New York, 1936); J. G. Frederick, *Standard Business Etiquette* (New York, 1937); Mildred M. Payne, *What Do I Do Now? A Guide to Correct Conduct and Dress for Business People* (New York, 1940); and Katharine Bleecker, *Business Etiquette; the A B C of Making Good* (New York, 1942).

[27] Hopkins, *Profits from Courtesy,* 4–6, 55, 87, 93.

CHAPTER VI. THE BALANCE SHEET

[1] Wilson, *Pocket Book of Etiquette* (originally published as *The New Etiquette: the Modern Code of Social Behavior,* copyright 1937 by Margery Wilson, here quoted by permission of J. B. Lippincott Company), 87.

[2] Without waiting for the future, Dorothy Dix ventured a prediction

in the *Boston Globe,* April 24, 1945, as to postwar marital manners: "The first war emancipated girls who scrapped the clinging-vine theory forever. This war emancipated the married women, and made the meek wife, who yes-yesed her husband and took whatever treatment he accorded her, as extinct as the Dodo. . . . She has proved that she can support herself and she is never going to be pushed around by any mere husband again." But, returning to the theme a year later (*Globe,* April 28, 1946), she viewed the situation somewhat differently, expressing apprehension about the "Problem Wife" intoxicated by her wartime "draught of freedom." Deploring this "new species of fauna," she wrote, "Now that Johnny has come back from the war they are finding it hard to put their necks back in the yoke. They still want to be free as no wife can be free. . . . This . . . is one of the main reasons why so many wives are getting divorces." She added darkly that, unless husbands and wives arrived at a satisfactory compromise, "the war will have been in vain, for we will have lost our country if we have broken up our homes."

[3] Anon., "Etiquette as a Civilizing Force," *World's Work,* XXVII (1913), 141. See also *Good Manners and Right Conduct,* issued by the Philippine Bureau of Education in 1917 as number 10 of *Civico-Educational Lectures.*

[4] The set included handbooks for Great Britain, Northern Ireland, West Africa, North Africa, Egypt, Syria, Iraq, Iran, India, Burma, the Netherlands East Indies, China, Korea, New Guinea, Australia, New Caledonia and New Zealand. There were also booklets for the occupation troops in Italy and Germany. Appropriately enough, the British *Good Housekeeping Magazine* and the American Office of War Information collaborated on *A Bride's Guide to the United States of America,* designed for English girls who married American soldiers.

[5] Emerson, *Works,* III, 135–136; VI, 163–166, 182, 185.

[6] Clapp, *Social Usage and Etiquette,* 13–14.

[7] Wilson, *Pocket Book of Etiquette* (originally published as *The New Etiquette: the Modern Code of Social Behavior,* copyright 1937 by Margery Wilson, here quoted by permission of J. B. Lippincott Company), 2.

[8] Anon., *Good Manners* (Philadelphia, 1870), 1–2.

[9] Francis Lieber, *Life and Letters* (T. S. Perry, ed., Boston, 1882), 314.

[10] Anon., "'Manner Is a Great Matter,'" *Century,* LXXXIII (1911), 311.

[11] F. D. Roosevelt, *Looking Forward* (New York, 1933), 266.

INDEX

Adams, Abigail, on Chesterfield, 12.
Alcott, W. A., on manners and morals, 19, 20; on servants, 82.
Allestree, Richard, book by, 6.
Almanacs, teach manners, 3.
American Museum, on manners, 13.
American Queen, on interest in etiquette, 32.
Ames, Nathaniel, on manners, 3.
Ancourt, d', Abbé, influence of, 6.
Appletons' Journal, on etiquette, 34.
Aristocracy, lack of hereditary, viii; desired, 1; rise of Southern, 6–7; "shoddy," 27–29.
Arthur, T. S., on manners, 19, 20.
Ashmore, Ruth. *See* Mallon, Isabel A.
Automobile, influences manners, 50.

Beadle, I. P., publisher, 22.
Bennet, John, advises women, 9, 10; on Chesterfield, 12, 78.
Bok, Edward, editor, 32.
Books of etiquette, colonial, 4–6, 8–9; pre-Civil War, 18–26; post-Civil War, 33–35; revise standards, 49; 1918–1945, 50–51; satirized, 58–59; for servicemen, 63–64; bibliographies of, 74–75.
Brathwaite, Richard, influence of, 6.
Brewster, William, owns etiquette manual, 5.
Business etiquette, 60–61.

Calling, etiquette of, 35, 40–41, 49.
Century Magazine, on manners, 49.
Chaperons, rise of, 44–45; opposed, 45–46; decline of, 46, 52, 54; in New Caledonia, 63–64.
Chapone, Hester M., book by, 9.
Chesterfield, Earl of, popular, 9, 12, 14, 79; precepts of, 11–12; condemned, 12, 78–79, 80; influence of, 64.
Children, taught manners, 4, 17, 31, 62, 76, 83–84.
Cities, society in, 30, 49, 65–66; chaperons in, 45, 46.
Clergy, refine manners, 3.
Cleveland, Grover, clean-shaven, 37–38; resents taunt, 42.
Cleveland, Rose E., etiquette writer, 33.
Clews, Henry, on new rich, 28.
Cobbett, William, on critics of manners, 75.
Conversation, Washington on, 5; women and, 7; Chesterfield on, 11; pre-Civil War, 24; post-Civil War, 35–37; after World War I, 56.
Cosmetics, frowned on, 10, 40; approved, 55.
Cotillion, rise and decline of, 44, 49, 52.
Courtship, colonial, 1–2; pre-Civil War, 25; post-Civil War, 44–47; after World War I, 54.

INDEX

Daisy Miller, influence of, 45, 46.
Dancing, W. S. Landor on, 19; attitude toward, 25, 43, 57–58, 86; ballroom, 28, 43–44, 57; informal, 57–58.
Debuts, rise of, 44, 52; decline, 56–57.
Dining etiquette, colonial, 5, 7, 11; pre-Civil War, 23–24; post-Civil War, 31, 41–43; after World War 1, 53, 56, 57; unsettled questions of, 66.
Dix, Dorothy. *See* Gilmer, Elizabeth M.
Dock, Christopher, instructs children, 76.
Dress, law prescribes, 2–3; Washington on, 5; Chesterfield on, 11. *See also* Fashions.
Drinking, increases, 50; by women, 55–56; cocktails, 56.

Education, in manners, 3–4, 17, 31, 62, 83–84; in business etiquette, 60–61.
Eichler, Lillian, influence of, 51; and new etiquette, 53; career of, 87, 88.
Eliot, C. W., on teaching manners, 84.
Emerson, R. W., philosopher of manners, 19, 67.
England, influences manners, 5–7, 9, 13, 65; influences fashions, 38.
Entertaining, simplified, 49, 56. *See also* Dancing, Dining.
Etiquette, general attitude toward, vii, 68; colonial, 1–14; pre-Civil War, 15–26; post-Civil War, 27–48; after World War I, 50–58; satirized, 58–59; business, 60–61; during World War II, 62–64; undecided points of, 66. *See also* Books of etiquette, Calling, Chaperons, Conversation, Courtship, Dancing, Dining etiquette, Drinking, Education, Entertaining, Fashions, Foreign influences, Magazines, Manners, Smoking, Society life.

Fairfax, Beatrice. *See* Manning, Marie.
Farrar, Eliza W., on manners, 19, 24; revised work of, 81.
Fashions, men's, 37–38, 49, 57; women's, 39–40. *See also* Dress.
Fern, Fanny. *See* Parton, Mrs. James.
Fitzhugh, William, on manners, 6.
Foreign influences, on manners, 4, 13, 29, 65; on dining, 23–24, 41–42; on dress, 38; on smoking, 39; on chaperonage, 45. *See also* England, France, Immigrants.
France, influences manners, 5, 13, 23–24, 29, 65.
Franklin, Benjamin, on morals and manners, 3, 8–9, 67, 77.

Gibson, C. D., caricatures society, 31.
Gilmer, Elizabeth M. (Dorothy Dix), advises women, 32; on postwar marital manners, 89–90.
Godey's Lady's Book, on manners, 17–18; on Chesterfield, 80.
Godkin, E. L., on manners, 29, 34; on fashions, 38.
Gregory, John, advises daughters, 9, 10; pleases Mrs. Adams, 12.
Gurowski, Adam de, on manners, 26.

INDEX

Hale, Sarah J., on manners, 18, 20.
Halifax, Lord, advises women, 6, 7.
Hall, Florence H., etiquette writer, 33.
Howells, W. D., author, 28.
Humorists, deride etiquette, 58–59, 89.

Immigrants, and manners, viii, 30, 69–70, 83.

Jackson, Andrew, rise of, 16; admired, 17.
James, Henry, influences etiquette, 45.
Jefferson, Thomas, owns etiquette book, 6.

Kenrick, William, etiquette writer, 9.

Ladies' Home Journal, advises girls, 32.
Ladies Library, influence of, 6; Franklin recommends, 9.
Landor, W. S., on dancing, 19.
Legislation, for manners, 1–3, 4, 13, 17, 31, 83.
Leslie, Eliza, on manners, 19.
Letter writing, advice on, 9, 75.
Lieber, Francis, quoted, 69.

McKinley, William, on smoking, 39.
Magazines, teach manners, 17–18, 31–32; print etiquette books, 33, 51.
Mallon, Isabel A. (Ruth Ashmore), advises girls, 32.
Manners, obstacles to acquiring, vii–viii; women influence, viii–ix; as morals, 1, 8, 19, 64; early attempts to refine, 3–7; desire for independence in, 13, 21; nationalism and democracy affect, 15–17; magazines and newspapers teach, 17–18, 31–32; as law, 22, 65; wealth affects, 27–30; migration affects, 30–31, 69–70; as art, 34–35, 65; World War I affects, 50–58, 62; diversity of foreign, 62–64; as pragmatism, 65; value of good, 67–69; national, 69–70; international, 70–71. *See also* Etiquette.
Manning, Marie (Beatrice Fairfax), advises women, 32.
Marriage, colonial attitude toward, 7, 10; Benjamin Franklin on, 8; pre-Civil War attitude toward, 25–26; post-Civil War, 47; World War affects, 90.
Mather, Cotton, on manners, 8, 67.
Moats, Alice L., on prohibition, 87.
Montez, Lola, on *The Arts of Beauty,* 19.
Moody, Eleazar, on manners, 4.
Morals, as manners, 1, 8, 19, 64; punishments for infringements of, 1–3; World War I affects, 50, 54–56.
Motion pictures, affect manners, 50.

New York statute of 1732, 4.
Newspapers, advertise etiquette books, 9; teach etiquette, 32, 51.

Ohio Practical Farmer, on manners, 31.

Parton, Mrs. James (Fanny Fern), on manners, 18, 20, 80.
Peacham, Henry, influence of, 6.
Petting, advice on, 54–55.

INDEX

Philippines, etiquette taught in, 62.
Pocket guides for servicemen, explain foreign usages, 63–64.
Poor Richard, maxims of, 3.
Post, Emily, influence of, 51; career of, 52; revises standards of etiquette, 52–53, 54; satirized, 58–59.
Prohibition, affects manners, 50.

Radio, influences manners, 50, 51.
Rogers, Will, on manners, 58–59.
Roosevelt, Alice, smokes, 39.
Roosevelt, F. D., on good-neighbor policy, 70–71.
Rural life, manners in, 46, 47, 66, 83; radio affects, 50.
Russians, influence dining, 41–42.

Sangster, Margaret E., etiquette writer, 33, 86.
School of Good Manners, instructs children, 4.
Scribner's Monthly, on manners, 31.
Sedgwick, Catharine M., encourages common folk, 16; on manners, 19, 20–21, 80.
Servant problem, before Civil War, 24, 81–82; after Civil War, 47.
Sherwood, Mary E. W. (Mrs. John), etiquette writer, 33.
Sigourney, Lydia H., on manners, 18–19.
Smoking, by men, 23, 38–39; by women, 39, 52–53, 55.
Society life, foreign influences on, 5–6, 9, 13, 38; influenced by democracy, 27–30; and debuts, 44, 52, 56–57; influenced by World War I, 50, 62. *See also* Dancing, Dining, Entertaining, Calling.
Soldiers, taught foreign etiquette, 62–64.
Sousa, J. P., composer, 44.
Speech, foreign influence on, 29; slang, 56, 63.

Tertullian, quoted, 8.
Tocqueville, Alexis de, on manners, 26.
Towne, C. W., humorist, 89.
Travelers, on women, ix, 45; on Southern society, 7; on marriage, 25; on manners, 26; appraised, 75.
Tuxedo, introduced, 38, 57.

Washington, George, draws up "Rules," 4–5, 76; acquires etiquette book, 6.
Wealth, increases after Civil War, 27–28, 83; affects manners, 28–30; affects dress, 39–40; affects dining, 41; antagonism to, 49; after World War I, 50.
Whiskers, rise and decline of, 37–38.
Whitefield, George, recommends book, 77.
Whole Duty of Man, The, influence of, 6; Franklin recommends, 9.
Willis, N. P., on American school of manners, 21.
Winthrop, John, Jr., owns etiquette book, 6.
Women, influence manners, viii–ix; foreigners' opinions of, ix, 45; colonial etiquette books for, 6–10; Chesterfield on, 11–12; magazines for, 17–18, 31–32; and servant problem, 24, 47, 81–82; increased independence of, 24–25, 49–50; newspapers advise,

32; smoke, 39, 52–53, 55; drink, 55–56; taught business etiquette, 60; treatment of foreign, 63. *See also* Chaperons, Courtship, Dress, Marriage.

World War I, affects manners and morals, 50–58, 62, 65.

World War II, foreign usages during, 62–64; influences women, 90.